IRENE SCHÖNE

KIEL. SAILING.CITY.

IRENE SCHÖNE

KIEL. SAILING.CITY.

OFFICIAL TRAVEL GUIDE

GMEINER

Mit freundlicher Unterstützung von:

Besuchen Sie uns im Internet:
www.gmeiner-verlag.de

Im Ehnried 5, 88605 Meßkirch
Telefon 0 75 75 / 20 95-0
info@gmeiner-verlag.de

1. Auflage 2023

Redaktion: Anja Sandmann
Layout / Herstellung, Umschlaggestaltung: Laura Stützle
unter Verwendung eines Bildes von © Irene Schöne (Cover),
© Kiel Marketing e. V. (U4)
Druck: AZ Druck und Datentechnik GmbH, Kempten
Printed in Germany
ISBN 978-3-8392-0433-7

CONTENTS

KIEL DISTRICTS

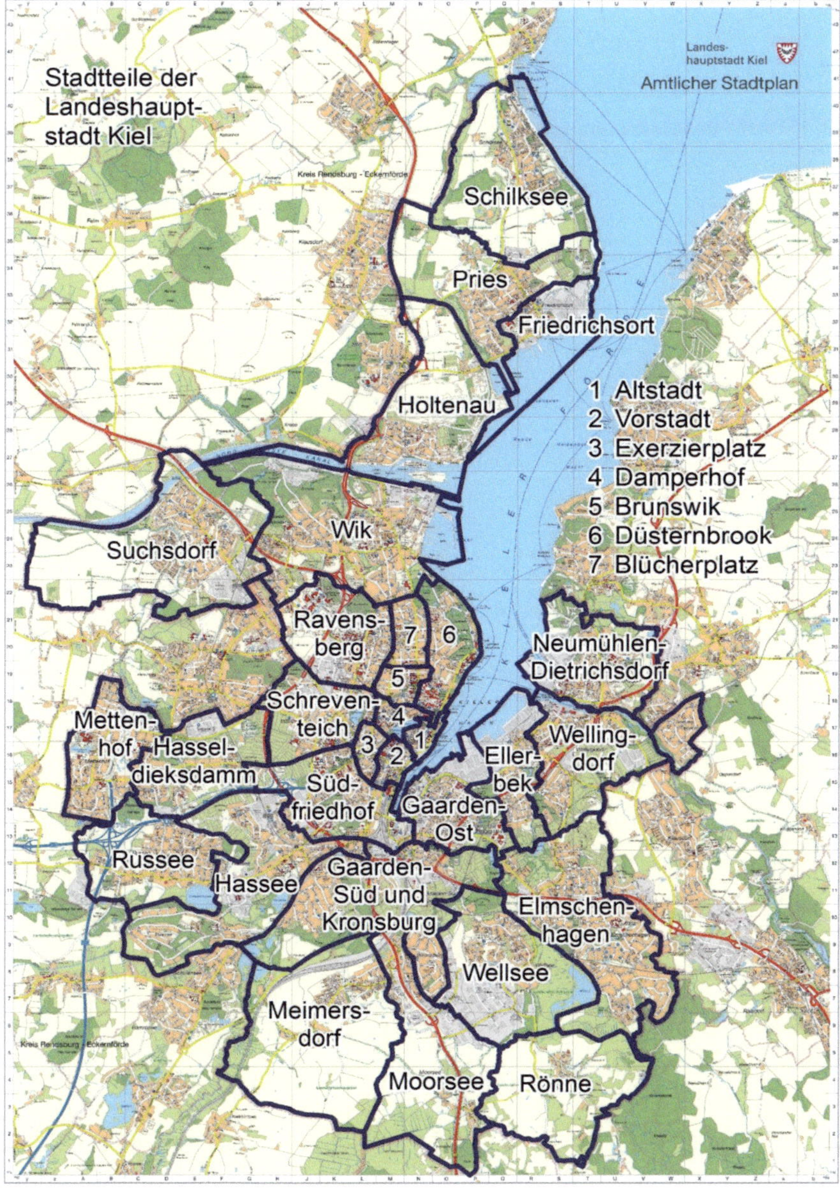

FOREWORD

Dear Reader,

This is Kiel's first-ever English-language tourist guide. It will give you more detailed information about our bustling city, the capital of Schleswig-Holstein, the northernmost of all sixteen German Bundesländer / federal states, and all the people and places associated with it.

Kiel is an attractive city offering a high standard of living, a city of science with world-known institutions, like the GEOMAR Helmholtz Centre for Ocean Research and the German National Leibniz Library of Economics (ZBW), the seat of the Schleswig-Holstein Parliament and government, as well as ship buildung and sports, with a majority of young people living here, and its four universities.

Today, people from 160 countries have made Kiel their home. And Kiel has always been and is an international city. Until 150 years ago, Kiel was connected to Denmark in personal union; the Russian Czar Peter III (1728–1762) was born in Kiel; in 1814 the Kiel Peace Treaty granted Norway independence from Denmark; and in 1946 the British Regional Commissioner Hugh Vivien Champion de Cresigny founded the modern federal state of Schleswig-Holstein. Today, daily ferry routes connect people with Norway, Sweden and the Baltic states.

While most of Kiel's attractions are to be found in the city centre, the surrounding districts of the capital city of Schleswig-Holstein also are worth a visit. We assume you would want to take a ferryboat trip from the harbour at the main station to explore the locks of Kiel Canal, the world's busiest artificial sea lane with all those huge ships, look for historic family roots or enjoy relaxig on its many beaches. A bus and ferryboat map is enclosed to help you get about.

This tourist guide helps connect you to our city, which has something for everyone. It contains information on Kiel's museums and its huge whale skeleton, its castle garden and the planetarium, as well as information about Kiel's universities, libraries and Nobel prize winners, architecture, music and opera performances, together with shopping experiences and where to get a good cup of freshly roasted coffee. We also strongly recommend a visit to Kiel's annual International Sailing Week, taking place every year in June, or its famous Christmas Market.

However, be prepared for a slight breeze. Kiel is next to the Baltic Sea, so there is always a light wind to enjoy, which is always welcome on hot summer days.

By the way, Kiel people are very polite. They thank bus drivers for their service by saying "Moin" when boarding.

And another speciality: Kiel is a very green city. Even 100 years ago, forward-thinking city planners connected the living districts with each other by installing green footpaths, planting trees, trees and more trees, so welcome today as they reduce the effects of climate change. We are sure you will be interested to read more about it.

We wish you a pleasant stay and interesting explorations.

Dr. Ulf Kämpfer

Lh Kiel - Pepe Lange

OB Dr. Kämpfer

KIEL'S LOCATION

Kiel, colloquially referred to as "tom kyle" ("on the wedge"), known as Chilonium in Roman times, is the capital of Schleswig-Holstein, the northernmost of Germany's federal states, situated to the south of Denmark, and being on the Baltic Sea, is the only German federal state capital directly on the coast.

Kiel sits at the southern end of a 17-kilometre-long fjord, open to the north, in a landscape shaped by the last ice age of 20 to 40-metre-high terminal moraines.

The fjord water is 10–13 metres deep, and is as deep as 27 metres near the "Ostseekai", and forms a natural seaport, the only one on the Baltic.

Kiel's latitude is 54°19'24", and its longitude 10°08'22".

Its highest point above sea level is 74.2 metres.

The red Kiel flag

KIEL'S PAST AND PRESENT

KIEL CONNECTS WITH THE UNITED KINGDOM OF GREAT BRITAIN AND NORTHERN IRELAND

In 1242, Kiel was granted city rights by Count Graf Adolf IV of Schauenburg, Holstein, Stormarn and Wagrien (1204–1261). Its coat of arms contains a nettle leaf and a boat.

The city was named "tom Kyle", meaning "at the wedge" (the Kiel Fjord is open to the north).

During a war against Denmark, Count Adolf promised God that if he won, he would establish a monastery and become a monk, and he lived in Kiel monastery until his death.

In 1318, Kiel received the right to mint its own money.

In 1283, Kiel joined the Hanse Baltic trading organisation, even though the town was not heavily engaged in it and did not utilise all of the benefits. The town never developed into one of the free "Hanse" towns as Lübeck or Hamburg did, and the "Hanse" expelled Kiel in 1554, arguing that Kiel had accommodated pirates.

The so-called Kieler Umschlag, an annual week-long market in January bringing together merchants and aristocrats from all over North Europe first mentioned in 1469, but presumably even older than that, was more important economically. The "Kieler Umschlag" money market ends with a public festival, re-established in 1975.

In 1838, industrialisation began with the establishment of the machine factory Schweffel & Howaldt.

Kiel in the 17th century, a photo of a print

After the German-Danish war in 1864, Schleswig-Holstein was governed by the victorious powers of Prussia and Austria, ending two years later, when Schleswig-Holstein became Prussian dominion. From 1867, the naval fleet of the Northern German Confederation was stationed in Kiel, with the German Emperor's fleet from 1871 on.

A sketch from the harbour by J. W. Carmichael shows Kiel's former profile. The sketch was printed in "The Illustrated London News", (1842–2003).

Kiel began to boom after Prussia's victory in the Franco-German war in 1871, and the first German national state was created, with the King of Prussia, Wilhelm I (1797–1888), its first emperor.

For more details on this era of Kiel's past, please contact "Maritimes Viertel", a registered association for history, culture and technology at Kiel-Canal,

Maritimes Viertel – Geschichte, Kultur und Technik am Kiel-Canal e. V.
Launched in 2012
Arkonastrasse 1
24106 Kiel-Wik
✆ 0151 40341850
www.maritimesviertel.de

Shipyards and a naval base were erected. Kiel became a "Reichskriegshafen" / imperial war port.

Former farmhouses were demolished, and multi-storey buildings erected containing large numbers of flats, especially on the east side of the fjord, for civil and military workers, with officers and civil servants, professors and businesspeople housed on the west side.

Around 1900, new flats were built, the first with inside toilets and lawns between them.

Then the Friedrich-Krupp-Germania Werft shipyard was installed (today the German Naval Yards, most recognisable by its more than 110-metre-high and 163-metre-long blue crane).

In 1914, before the outbreak of World War I, there were 32,000 military staff living in Kiel. About 33,000 people worked at the shipyards, meaning that 75 % of people derived their in-

Privat property

come from the Navy and ship building industry.

Due to the city's military importance, Kiel was nearly totally destroyed by Allied bombings in World War II. And it was during this time that Kiel even had a connection to Hollywood. James M. Stewart (1908–1997), the iconic US film actor, interrupted his successful Hollywood career to join the US Air Force in 1941, and his first mission as a pilot was on 13 December 1943, bombing submarine building yards in a B-24 "Liberator".

During War II, a total of 240 ships were sunk in Kiel's fjord.

Kiel became capital of Schleswig-Holstein when the new federal state was established on 23 August 1946 by Hugh Vivian Champion de Crespigny, the High Commissioner of the British Military Command. In 2016, the last British forces left Kiel.

On 15 September 2021, the International Day of Democracy, Schleswig-Holstein's Parliament and "Schleswig-Hostein's Sparkassen"/public saving banks honoured the United Kingdom with a prize to commemorate its role in the founding of the new German democracy.

After World War II, the city needed to re-invent itself – just like the British town of Coventry, which had been heavily bombed by the German air force. It was a time when British and German people came together in a spirit of peace building. A hall in Gaarden was named after Coventry to commemorate the atrocities people on both sides had suffered.

Historians are therefore right to claim that Kiel was founded not just once, but three times: in 1242, 1865 and most recently in 1946.

Even today, 75 years after the end of World War II, unexploded munition is still present in Kiel's soil and water: In Kiel's outer fjord, there are lots of corroding bomb remains and munitions. This could cause a great deal of damage, as their steel mantles are now dissolving. Experts estimate that 1.6 million tons of war munitions are in the North and the Baltic Sea and need to be defused.

In 2020 alone, four unexploded bombs had to be removed in the city centre.

KIEL PEACE

KIEL CONNECTS WITH NORWAY

On 14 January 1814, at the end of the Napoleonic wars, after the Swedish crown prince Bernadotte had conquered fortress "Friedrichsort", in Kiel in the "Buchwald'scher Hof" the peace treaty was signed between Denmark, Sweden and Great Britain. Denmark was obliged to give Norway to Sweden.

At the end of February of the same year, Norway declared independence from Sweden, and subsequently passed a new constitution on 17 May, an event which is commemorated by a stone pillar in the "Dänische Strasse" (the building was destroyed in an air raid in 1944).

In 1848 an independent government for Schleswig-Holstein was acclaimed at the "Alter Markt" in Kiel. However, the town was still under the control of the Danish monarchy.

Citizens had held demonstrations to demand more freedom and less

Memorial to the 1848 Revolution

arbitrary princely rule in Germany's dukedoms and free cities. In 1849, the first German Constitution was agreed,

Stone pillar "Kiel Peace of 1814"

and in due course the first German national state formed.

On 3 November 1918, during World War 1, sailors and labourers went on strike. They held no hope of a victory. In their opinion, the war was already lost. Thousands of Kiel residents demonstrated for better food rations. When the admiralty ignored their demand, a revolt ensued. Seven mariners were shot and 29 injured in the revolt's suppression.

With their demonstration, the brave sailors laid the foundation for Germany's first democracy, commonly known as the "Weimar Republic". The Nazis' ascent to power in 1933 however ended democracy in Germany.

British War Commonwealth Cemetery

ihs

After the end of World War II, a British Commonwealth War Cemetery was erected close to the German military cemetery, at "Nordfriedhof" at "Westring". Here, almost 1,000 fallen British Commonwealth soldiers, from Great Britain, Canada, Australia, New Zealand, as well as from Poland were laid to rest. The area is designed by the British architect Philip Hepworth.

Kiel War Cemetery is maintained by the Commonwealth War Graves Commission, which maintains all British cemeteries around the world. The organisation also provides information on the names of the soldiers and the location of their graves.

In 1996, the artist Gunter Demnig initiated an art project called Stolpersteine / stumbling blocks, in cooperation with the German Society for Christian-Jewish Cooperation. Brass blocks were dug into pavements engraved with the names of victims of the Nazi regime who had lived there. A total of 270 blocks, 10 × 10 cm in size, have been installed to preserve their eternal memory. The project was financed through charitable donations. Today, you can find more than 80,000 blocks across Germany commemorating victims and where they once lived.

In Kiel, there are for example three stumbling stones sitting at the corner of Feldstrasse and Yorckstrasse in the Blücherplatz district remembering the Abramowicz family who lived there: Leon, born in 1893, his wife Else, born in 1891, Narwa, Estonia, and their daughter Minna Lotte, born in 1927. In 1933, the family took refuge in France, they were interned in Drancy, France, and in 1942 they were deported to Auschwitz, where they were murdered.

Three stumbling stones commemorating the Abramowicz family

MONASTERY AND CARILLON

Near the "Alte Markt", there are the ruins of a Franciscan monastery named "Zu unserer Lieben Frau" ("To our dear Lady"), built during the reign of Kiel's founder, Count Adolf IV of Schauenburg, who became a monk after the battle of Bornhöved. The monastery was dissolved in 1530 following the Reformation.

Today it is partly used to house students and the elderly, and in the summer months there is a café in the garden in the city centre.

In 1999, a carillon was installed in the tower of the former monastery and extended in 2005 to hold a total of 50 bronze bells. It is played on the first Saturday of each month at 12 pm, 3 pm and 6 pm, starting with the chorale "Verleih uns Frieden" ("In Thy Mercy Grant Us Peace") by the German composer Felix Mendelssohn Bartholdy (1809–1947).

ihs

Kiel Monastery

A SELECTION OF KIEL'S PLACES OF WORSHIP

In the north of Germany, the majority of people are Lutheran Protestants. So, it is not astonishing that Lutheran churches constitute the majority of Kiel's churches. A selection of Kiel's churches can be found below:

St. Nikolai Church with the Ernst Barlach (1870–1938) sculpture "Der Geisteskämpfer" / "Spiritual Warrior" standing in front, depicting the victory of good over evil

Ancient fresco

St. Nikolai Church: Built at the "Alter Markt" in the 13th century, the historic centre of Kiel's old town, originally Catholic and named after Saint Nicholas, the pa-

Part of the bronze font Johann Apegeter, 1344

tron saint of seafarers. Destroyed in World War II, it was rebuilt in 1950 by the architect Gerhard Langmaack. Its bronze font dates from 1344 and was built by Hans Apengeter.

Its three-winged altar is from a graduate of the Lübeck School (about 1460). Because of its fragile state, it is only exhibited for a limited period each year. The frescoes over the top of the side entrance are even older.

St. Nikolai Church
Alter Markt
24103 Kiel-Altstadt
✆ 0431 95008
www.st-nikolai-kiel.de

The **University Church** was erected in a triangle shape, a symbol of the trinity of God by architects Kettner and Weitling in 1965.

niversity Church, uilt on the trinity rinciple

ihs

Petrus Church

ihs

University Church
Westring / Ecke Olshausenstrasse
24118 Kiel-Ravensberg
✆ 0431 88000
www.esg-kiel.de

The **Petrus Church** at "Anscharpark" was built between 1905 and 1907 by Karl Moser and Robert Curjel as a garrison church. The oak roof is designed as a ship hull ("Kiel oben") with interesting art deco windows in its west front. Famous for its unique acoustics, the church is today mostly used for concerts.

Petrus Church
Weimarer Strasse /
Ecke Adalbertstrasse
24106 Kiel-Wik
✆ 0431 348 64
www.petrus-kirche.eu

Bethlehem Church in "Friedrichsort" was built in 1875 for the garrison and is a listed building. The church is Kiel's third oldest and was built to replace the garrison church inside the former Danish fortress of "Friedrichsort", built in 1632, which over the years turned out to be too small.

The building is totally constructed of wood, indeed with the altar pointing to the wrong side, which is to the West. Two centuries ago in Prussia, there was a strict seating arrangement: the military sitting separately from civilians, the officers with their wives occupying the front seats.

Bethlehem Church
Interessengemeinschaft Bethlehem Kirche e. V.
Möhrkenstrasse 9
24159 Kiel-Friedrichsort
✆ 0431 391038
www.bethlehem-kirche.de

There are three different **mosques** in Kiel, offering services which can be attended. Please contact them directly for more information.

SCHURA Islamische Religionsgemeinschaft Schleswig-Holstein e. V.

Bethlehem Church

ihs

President Mr Fatih Mutlu
Alte Lübeckerchaussee 19
24113 Kiel
✆ 0431 65991571
www.schurash.de

Kiel Synagogue, in a listed building in Waitzstrasse 43, is where the Jewish community worships today. The Synagogue was originally situated in Goethestrasse 13, 24116 Schrevenpark. Today, the site is marked by a memorial stone, as the synagogue was plundered and devastated by the Nazi SS and SA organisations on Kristallnacht on 9 November 1938, and then demolished.

Jüdische Synagoge und Gemeindezentrum
Waitzstrasse 43
24105 Kiel-Düsternbrook
✆ 0431 6575030
www.jgemeindekiel@yahoo.de

Kiel's **Old Jewish Cemetery** is situated at Michelsenstrasse, circa 250 metres east of "Südfriedhof". It is about 2,000 square metres wide and still used as burial place, but is not open to the public.

Old Jewish Cemetery
Michaelsenstrasse
24114 Kiel

ihs

The old Jewish Cemetery

KIEL CASTLE AND CASTLE GARDEN

KIEL CONNECTS WITH DENMARK

The foundation of Kiel Castle dates back to 1242, while the first house was erected in 1512 by Denmark's King Friedrich I.[1]

Kiel Castle, a one-time residence of the Gottorf dukes, was built between 1558–1568 in the Renaissance style. The castle and the old town were situated on an island, and until 1685, there was a water ditch between the castle and the castle garden through which the "Kleiner Kiel" / Little Kiel lake was connected to the north side of the Kiel fjord.

In 1665, it was the founding place of Kiel's Christian Albrecht University.

Queen Sophia of Mecklenburg, widow of Danish King Friedrich II, renovated the dilapidated castle in around 1610. Another member of the Danish royal family, Friedrike Amalie, daughter of the Danish King Friedrich III and wife of the founder of Kiel's university, Christian Albrecht, appointed famous Swiss architect Dominicus Pelli to plan the castle's expansion.

ihs

Kiel Castle, Pelli build

1 Further information can be found at www.freundeskreis-kielerschloss.de

ihs

Kiel Castle: Pelli building on the left and the white "Landeshalle" with tower at the back

KIEL CONNECTS WITH RUSSIA

From 1727, Anna Petrowna, oldest daughter of the Russian Czar Peter the Great and wife of Duke Carl Friedrich of Holstein-Gottorf, lived in the castle and died here in 1728 after giving birth to her son Carl Peter Ulrich of Holstein-Gottorf.

In 1745, Carl Peter Ulrich married the German Princess Sophie Auguste von Anhalt-Zerbst-Dornburg, born 1729 in Stettin.

Carl Peter Ulrich became Russia's Czar Peter III in 1762, but only for six months.

After his death, his wife Sophie Auguste became Czarina Catherine II the Great, reigning until 1796.

Carl Peter Ulrich is the founder of the House of Romanov-Holstein-Gottorf, which ruled Russia until 1917.

Peter Horree / Alamy Stock Photo

"Czarina Catherine II" the Great

Statue of Duke Carl Peter Ulrich von Holstein-Gottorf, 1728–1762 by Alexa Taratynov, in front of the Rantzau- / P building of Kiel Castle

One year after becoming czarina, Catherine II commissioned the restoration of Kiel Castle by the architect Sonnin, and had the university built close to the castle. There is a memorial in the south part of the castle commemorating this.

From 1838, another daughter of a Danish king, Wilhelmine of Denmark, lived in Kiel castle together with her family for about 25 years.

And in 1848, after the first German revolution, Kiel Castle housed the first democratically elected assembly of Schleswig-Holstein. It passed what was then the most progressive and liberal constitution in any German state.

After the German-Danish war (1 February to 30 October 1864), Kiel was a divided town for a period of nine months. Then Schleswig-Holstein became independent from Denmark and a province of Prussia. Austrian Field Marshal Freiherr Ludwig von Gablenz resided in the castle. Kiel's bridge to the east side of the fjord is named after him.

From 1888 on, Prince Heinrich, brother of the German Kaiser Wilhelm II (1859–1941) and grandson of the British Queen Victoria, lived here with his family. His wife, Irene, was a sister of Alexandra, the last empress of Russia.

Most of Kiel Castle was destroyed during World War II and was rebuilt in the Sixties by the architects Sprotte and Neve, only the original building by Domenico Pelli is still standing.

The water feature between the original building and the new building was created in 1966 by Ulrich Beier.

KIEL CASTLE GARDEN

Opened in 1838 and designed in the style of a romantic English park, the

"Schlossgarten" stretches from the castle in the south to Kiel's Kunsthalle art museum in the north.

It features a statue, erected in 1896 by Adolf Brütt, of Wilhelm Friedrich Ludwig of the House of Hohenzollern (1797–1888), later King Wilhelm I of Prussia, who freed Schleswig-Holstein from Danish domination in the 1864 German-Danish war, resulting in its incorporation into Prussia in 1867.

Following unification in 1871, Wilhelm I was proclaimed first emperor of the German Empire.

For more detailed information about Kiel's history as well as lectures and excursions, please contact:

Gesellschaft für Kieler Stadtgeschichte e. V.
Fleethörn 9
24103 Kiel
✆ 0170 00971022
www.kieler-stadtgeschichte.de

ihs

Kiel Castle Garden: Emperor Wilhelm I

MUSEUMS AND MUSEUM HARBOUR

Kiel has a lot of interesting museums. Please note that all museums are closed on Mondays.

Flandern Bunker

The **Computermuseum** is Germany's third-largest computer museum. It was founded in 2011 in an old bunker in the district of Neumühlen-Dietrichsdorf. Its exhibits include a "Z11" by Zuse KG and the "Siemens 2002", as well as the 1.6-ton "Cyber 76".

Computermuseum
Eichenbergskamp 8
24149 Kiel-Neumühlen-Dietrichsdorf
✆ 0431 2101741
www.computermuseum-kiel.de

ihs

Open Air Museum Molfsee (entrance)

The **Flandernbunker,** a relic of World War II, was originally built in 1944 for the submarine command. It is 11 metres tall with 2.5-metre-thick walls. It was opened to the public in the post-war years, and is under the stewardship of Verein Mahnmal Kilian e.V.

Flandernbunker
Kiellinie 249
24105 Kiel-Düsternbrook
✆ 0431 2606309
www.mahnmalkilian.de

The **Freilichtmuseum**/Open-Air Museum Molfsee is situated a bit south of Kiel. It exhibits the cultural history of rural Schleswig-Holstein, with 60 farmhouses, barns and rural workshops from the 16th to the 20th century, as well as exhibitions about Schleswig-Holstein's history, across 40 hectares.

Freilichtmuseum Molfsee
Hamburger Landstrasse 97
24113 Molfsee
✆ 0431 6596622
www.freilichtmuseum-sh.de

The **Industrial Museum** opened on the site of a former metal foundry in 2007. It was originally built in 1884 and is the oldest existing factory of Kiel's shipbuilding industry. It was operated by the Howaldtswerke until 1980.

Industrial Museum, Kiel-Neumühlen

ihs

Verein Industriemuseum Howaldtsche Metallgiesserei
Grenzstrasse 1
24149 Kiel-Neumühlen-Dietrichsdorf
✆ 0431 9013466

The **Kanalmuseum** hosts an exhibition about the history of the Kiel Canal, the so-called "blue band" running through Schleswig-Holstein. Built at the end of the 19th century, it is the world's busiest artificial waterway.

Kanalmuseum
Arkonastrasse 1
24106 Kiel-Wik
www.nok-sh.de/freizeittipps/museum-am-kanal.html

Public Art Gallery "Kunsthalle"

ihs

The **Kunsthalle**/Art Museum was founded in 1843 by Peter Wilhelm Forchhamer and its building was constructed in 1909 by Georg Lohr. It hosts a special collection of paintings of artists from the Netherlands and local artists, as well as an antique collection.

Kunsthalle
Düsternbrooker Weg 1
24105 Kiel-Düsternbrook
✆ 0431 8805756
www.kunsthalle-kiel.de

The **Landesgeschichtliche Sammlung** of the Schleswig-Holsteinische Landesbibliothek / Schleswig-Holstein State Library, established in 1895, is the central library for Schleswig-Holstein and its history and culture.

Landesgeschichtliche Sammlung of the Schleswig-Holsteinische Landesbibliothek
Wall 47 / 51
24103 Kiel-Altstadt
✆ 0431 6967710
www.shlb.de

If you are interested in archaeology, one of the **largest Megalith cemeteries** in Europe was discovered in Flintbek, in the south of Kiel. It is called the "Flintbek Sickle" and is 4 kilometres long and 500 metres wide. It was excavated between 1976 and 1996. Archaeologists have found from C14-analysis that the wheel traces at Flintbek are more than 5,400 years old. This has led some scientists to conclude that the wheel was not invented in the Middle East as it was previously thought, but in central Europe.

Maschinenmuseum
Am Kiel Kanal 44
24106 Kiel-Wik
✆ 0431 5943450
www.maschinenmuseum-kiel-wik.de

Kiel's University of Applied Sciences has an observatory and, close to it, a so-called **Mediendom**, a domed theatre with interesting programmes showing 360-degree films on astronomical and scientific themes. Children love it!

Mediendom
Sokratesplatz 6
24149 Kiel-Neumühlen-Dietrichsdorf
✆ 0431 2101741
www.fh-kiel.de

The "Mediendc

ihs

The **Medizin- und Pharmaziehistorische Sammlung** der Christian-Albrechts-Universität / Christian Albrecht University Museum of Medicine and Pharmacy was designed by Martin Gropius (uncle of Walter Gropius, the founder of the Bauhaus architectural movement).

Medizin- und Pharmaziehistorische Sammlung der Christian-Albrechts-Universität
Brunswiker Str. 2
24103 Kiel-Brunswik
✆ 0431 8805721
www.med-hist.uni-kiel.de

Mineralogisch-Petrographisches und Geologisch-Paläontologisches Museum
Ludewig-Meyn-Strasse 10–12
24118 Kiel-Ravensberg
✆ 0431 8802905
www.ifg.uni-kiel.de

The small **Ofenmuseum** / stove museum hosts many interesting historic stoves, showing how rooms were heated before the days of central heating systems.

Ofenmuseum
Hans-Günter Fahrenkrug
Eichenbergskamp 14–16
24149 Kiel-Dietrichsdorf
✆ 0431 204060
www.ofenmuseum-kiel.de

The **Schifffahrtsmuseum** / the former fish auction hall was built in 1909 according to plans of the architect Georg Pauly, and is situated outdoors, at the quay where the old ferry boat "Stadt Kiel" is moored. It can be booked for private parties.

ihs

The Schifffahrtsmuseum, once a fish hall, today a maritime museum

Schifffahrtsmuseum
Wall 65
24103 Kiel-Vorstadt
✆ 0431 9013428
www.schifffahrtsmuseum-kiel.de

... as can the old steamship **Bussard**, the last barrel stacker, launched in 1906, operated by Dampfer Bussard e. V.

Dampfer Bussard e. V.
Hofholzallee 171
24109 Kiel-Hasseldieksdamm
✆ 0431 555587
www.dampfschiff-bussard.de

The **Theatergeschichtliche Sammlung und Hebbel-Sammlung** / Historical Museum of Theatre and Hebbel Collection is currently more of an archive than a museum. It opened in 1924, with the Hebbel Collection being added in 1926. The collection is named after Friedrich Hebbel (1813–1863), a famous German author, and contains, for example, theatre engravings from the Renaissance to the present, stage designs for Wagner operas by Schinkel and Döll, approximately 300 contemporary photographs of the Deutsche Theater in Berlin, a gift from Max Reinhardt, Hans Holtorf's portfolios of Shakespearean comedies, set models and costume designs by Gottfried Pilz, and other historic material.

Theatergeschichtliche Sammlung und Hebbel-Sammlung
Viewings by appointment
Leibnizstrasse 8
24118 Kiel-Ravensberg
✆ 0431 8803410
www.museen-sh.de

The Kiel **Ethnological Museum** was founded in 1884, when Kiel mariners brought back exhibits from their journeys to the south which had never been seen before.

Warleberger Hof
City Museum

Völkerkunde Museum
Hegewischstrasse 3
24105 Kiel-Brunswik
✆ 0431 8805000
www.universitätssammlungen.de/sammlung/239

Kiel's **Stadtmuseum Warleberger Hof**, a municipal museum, with rotating exhibitions of the city's archaeology and presentations of Kieler Kunstkeramik, is a former aristocratic residence, built in 1616, with an entrance door dating from 1765.

Stadtmuseum Warleberger Hof
Dänische Strasse 19
24103 Kiel-Altstadt
✆ 0431 9013425
www.kiel.de

The **Zoologisches Museum**/Zoological Museum, built in 1881, was one of the first of its kind, with the most extensive whale bone collection in Germany and a 14-metre-long whale skeleton, installed by the German zoologist Karl August Möbius (1825–1908).

Zoologisches Museum
Hegewischstrasse 2
24105 Kiel-Brunswik
✆ 0431 8805170
www.zoologisches-museum.uni-kiel.de

The **Museumshafen**/Museum Harbour, opposite Kiel's main station, was built in 2004 as part of the new construction of the "Hörn". Traditional sailing ships and historic watercraft are

A whale skeleton in the Zoological Museum

ihs

moored here. The non-profit organisation Museumshafen Kiel e.V. aims to preserve and restore them. Some of the boats can be booked for private parties.

Museumshafen Kiel e. V.
Am Germaniahafen
24143 Kiel-Gaarden
✆ 0151 52133309
www.museumshafen-germaniahafen-kiel.de

With interesting traditional sailing ships like the 115-year-old Kiel-Marstal schooner "Zuversicht", under the protection of the **Verein Jugendsegeln**, laid down in 1905 and converted into a sailing ship in 1980, it is now used for youth training under the supervision of Verein Jugendsegeln e.V.

Verein Jugendsegeln e.V.
Halle 36
Holzkoppelweg 33
24118 Kiel-Ravensberg
✆ 0431 3640586 (AB)
www.verein-jugendsegeln.de

ihs

Museum Harbour

CULTURAL MEETING PLACES – PAST AND PRESENT

The **Forsteck Villa** was built in 1895 by Heinrich Adolph Meyer (1822–1889) and his wife Marie in the grounds of today's Dietrichsen Park in the Düsternbrook district, a large villa erected in the "Gründerzeit" style. It was heavily damaged in 1944 by bombing during World War II and later demolished.

Meyer was a manufacturer of walking sticks, and later became a politician. He was a Member of the Reichstag for the "Deutsche Fortschrittspartei", and especially interested in oceanography. He published books on the subject.

Forsteck Villa became a cultural meeting place, where poets, composers and musicians met, for example, the poet Theodor Fontane, who wrote a poem about the house, called "Forsteck", the author Klaus Groth, the pianist Clara Schumann and the composer Johannes Brahms, and even the then US Secretary of the Interior, Carl Schurz.

The timber-framed house for the inspector of the old Botanical Garden is

ihs

Schleswig-Holstein's Literature House

today used as **Schleswig-Holstein's Literature House,** with readings and lectures held by different authors.

Literature House in the Old Botanical Garden
Schwanenweg 13
24105 Kiel-Düsternbrook
✆ 0431 5796840
www.literaturhaus-sh.de

The **Hans Kock Stiftung,** a former aristocratic estate, and the children's republic with Willy Brandt, former German chancellor, participating:

What is today the estate of the Hans Kock foundation Gut Seekamp was first mentioned in 1350, and hundred years later got into the possession of the Rantzau family. In 1626, it was sold to King Christian IV of Denmark and

Hans Kock Stiftung

Norway, who erected the sea fortress Friedrichsort.

It is said that in 1615, two women, Engelke Krabbbenhöft and Abelke Kohberg, were accused of witchcraft and executed there.

Auguste Wried, mother of the painter Hans Olde (1855–1917), the most famous of the North German impressionists, was born here. Olde's own son Hans "the younger" (1895–1987) also became a well-known painter. In 1925, he sold most of the land to Kiel city.

The estate saw many famous guests, among them the impressionist Lovis Corinth and the Kiel born poet Detlef von Liliencron, the sculptor Adolf Brütt and Alfred Lichtwark, the founder of modern museum education.

In 1927, the journalist Andreas Gayk of the "Schleswig-Holsteinische Volkszeitung" and later Lord Mayor of Kiel, proclaimed here the first free German "children's republic", one of the German youth camps, for 2,300 children from working-class families to offer them a chance learning how democracy is working. Kiel was the most important of all the 30 children's republics in Germany. Former German chancellor Willy Brandt of the Social Democratic party and 1971 Nobel Peace Prize Laureate (1913–1992) participated as a young boy and gave here his first radio interview.

In 1986, the sculptor Hans Kock (1924–2007), whose wife Anna (b. Olde) was born on the estate, established together with the city of Kiel the Hans Kock foundation in order to create a contemporary cultural center for the arts. Kock donated twelve of his larger sculptural works and transformed the former agricultural estate by landscaping the park into a refined synthesis of nature and art.

Today, in cooperation with the "Bürgerinitiative Kulturpark Seekamp" exhibitions, meetings and talks are taking place in summer.

Hans Kock Stiftung
Seekamper Weg 10
24159 Kiel-Schilksee
✆ 0431 38008888
www.hans-kock-stiftung.de
and
www.kulturpark-seekamp.de

FORTRESS FRIEDRICHSORT

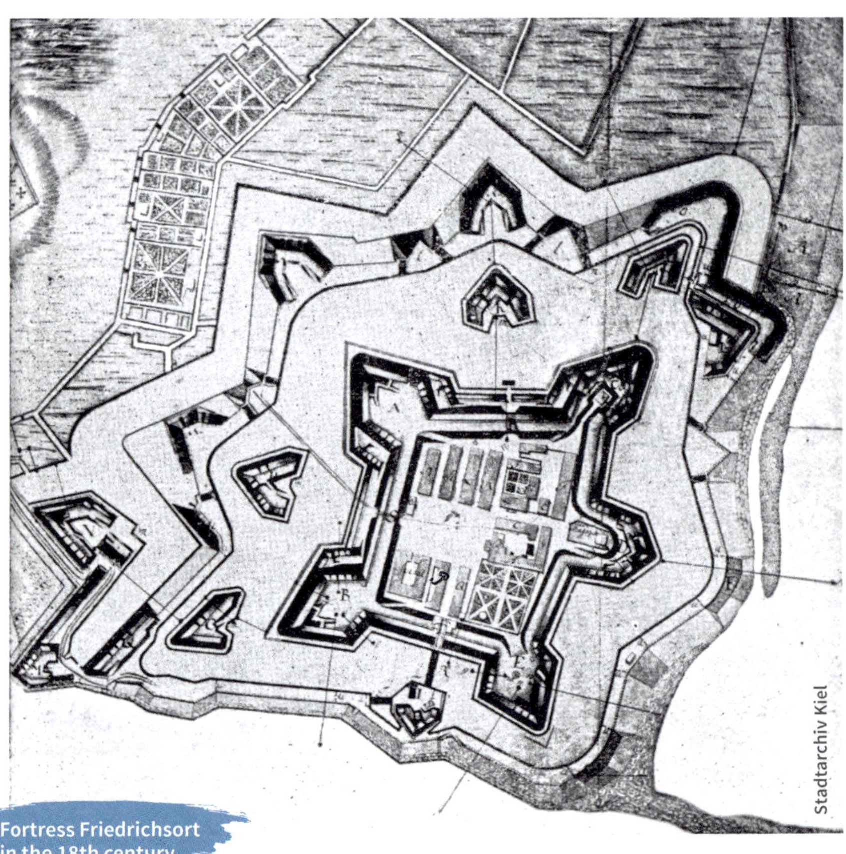

Stadtarchiv Kiel

Fortress Friedrichsort in the 18th century

Fortress Friedrichsort, in the district of the same name, is a former Danish fortification situated on the west of the Kiel Fjord at its narrowest point, north of Kiel Canal. It is Germany's only sea fortress and is a listed building. It measures 300 metres in diameter.

The fortress was built in 1632 by the Danish King Christian IV to protect the town during the Thirty Years War against Sweden. It was given the name "Christianspries".

However, the Swedish conquered it in 1643, and it was destroyed by the Danish King Friedrich III in 1648. Reconstruction began in 1663.

Swedish forces conquered it again in 1813 during the Napoleon Wars, after which it was finally liberated under the "Treaty of Kiel" on 14 January 1814.

During the Schleswig-Holstein uprising in 1848, Kiel citizens occupied the Danish fortress which was under the command of the Prussian officer Werner Siemens (later Werner von Siemens, the electrical engineer, inventor and industrialist, 1816–1892). Together with chemist professor Carl Himly, Siemens later invented the electrically charged sea mine. These mines protected Kiel and prevented Danish troops from moving their ships into the fjord.

When the dukedom became a Prussian province in 1867 after the German-Danish war, the fortress was extended.

The fortress had to be dismantled after World War I, but was used again by the German navy after 1935. Most of its buildings were subsequently destroyed in World War II.

Kiel City Council is working on plans to reconstruct this unique historic site and open the fortress to the public.

For more information or a visit, please contact:

Verein der Freunde der Festung Friedrichsort e. V.
Koloniestrasse 6
24159 Kiel-Friedrichsort
✆ 0431 556352
www.festung-friedrichsort.org

Close by, on Kiel fjord's narrowest part, stands Friedrichsort lighthouse, warning ships of the sandbank

ESTABLISHING DEMOCRACY

FROM KIEL TO THE WHOLE OF GERMANY

With the end of World War I in sight, sailors and labourers refused to continue fighting. The sailor Karl Artelt and the shipyard worker Lothar Popp, both members of the "Unabhängige Sozialdemokratische Partei Deutschlands"/Independent Social Democratic Party of Germany, organised demonstrations of several thousand Kiel inhabitants, demanding peace and bread. Seven demonstrators were shot dead and 29 were wounded. More soldiers were transferred to Kiel to smash the revolt, but some soldiers even changed sides, and they did not give up, as their situation was intolerable. They set up a workers' and soldiers' council to govern Kiel, and thereby triggered Germany's second democratic revolution, on 3 November 1918, which then spread throughout Germany. People's demands included the release of all political prisoners, personal freedom and freedom of speech, abolition of censorship, and the withdrawal of troops.

Memorial Plate commemorating the events of November 1918

A memorial plaque commemorates the events of November 1918 (translated): In this very building, Legienstrasse 22–24, 24103 Kiel-Altstadt, at the beginning of November 1918, the Kiel Workers' and Soldiers' Council held a meeting. From this building, on 9 November 1918, the decisive initiative came to proclaim the first German republic in Berlin.

Germany's first revolution had taken place in 1848. The revolutionaries' aim was to establish a German nation state, a constitutional monarchy, to replace the existing Confederation of 39 independent German principalities, to formulate a liberal constitution, establish a Parliament and abolish serfdom once and for all. However, it failed to separate the city from the Danish monarchy.

The Olshausen brothers, Justus and Theodor, played an important role in the 1848 revolt. A road in Kiel is named after them, close to Christian Albrecht University.

Justus Olshausen, born in 1800, was the first vice president of the Kiel constitutional assembly.

Theodor, born in 1802, was a journalist, and having studied law, he became a member of the provisional government in Kiel. Theodor demanded that Schleswig-Holstein be freed from the Danish monarchy. In 1851, he was forced to leave Kiel and fled to the United States of America. There, he became owner of two newspapers, "Der Demokrat" and "Westliche Post". This shows that, at the time, many people of German descent must have lived in St. Louis, Missouri. In a letter to his brother dated 18 April 1864, he wrote (translated):

A different reason to return to Germany could have been the Schleswig-Holstein case. In the middle of December, I received an invitation from half a dozen old Holstein democrats to

Olshausen Brothers memorial

ihs

come back, as they needed leadership. It was, however, very clear for me that things would take the same direction as in 1848, because people would again cling to the Duke of Augustenburg and the German aristocrats, and that there would be no possibility of changing that, due to the usual blind trust in Germany. If it is not possible to act radically, it is better to abstain.

The 1918 revolution brought an end to the German Empire and the rule of the Hohenzollern family. Aristocrats were stripped of their privileges and titles. The Hohenzollern Kaiser Wilhelm II (1859–1941), grandson of Britain's Queen Victoria, was forced to abdicate and to retreat into exile.

The Kiel "mutiny", as it was sometimes called, led to the establishment of the so-called Weimar Republic. Now every man and woman had, besides others, the right to vote, with women having this right for the first time in Germany.

In August 1919, the new republican constitution came into force, and Germany's first democracy was born.

However, influential right-wing forces wanted to restore the monarchy or install an authoritarian dictatorship. "On 13 March 1920, the Erhardt naval brigade moved into Berlin. Under the leadership of General Walther von Lüttwitz and the right-wing politician Wolfgang Kapp, the Reich government under Chancellor Gustav Bauer (SPD) was disposed. It triggered the Reich government's order to disband the reactionary Ehrhardt Naval Brigade and the Loewenfeld Freikorps in order to implement the disarmament provisions of the Versailles Peace Treaty.

Trade unions called a general strike, which was not only supported by the workers, but also by large sections of

Memorial to the 1918 revolution, created by the artist Hans Jürgen Breuste, erected in 1982

ihs

the middle classes. On 17 March 1920, the usurpers were forced to give up. Most of the protagonists of the putsch remained unpunished and were able to continue their struggle against the republic." 76 Kiel citizens were killed and 200 wounded, as is said on the information chart which stands today at the corner of Bergstrasse / Jensendamm.

Seven years later, in 1927, a so-called "children's republic" at Gut Seekamp was established by the journalist Andreas Gayk (please compare chapter "Cultural Meeting Places"), to enable children how to participate in democracy.

This forward-thinking initiative was destroyed by then rising Nazi party. The German Federal Parliament lost its power when, on 30 January 1933, Austrian-born Adolf Hitler was appointed chancellor by Paul von Hindenburg, the second German president.

1920 Kapp-Putsch memorial

One of the most important resistance groups against the rise of the "Nationalsozialistische Partei" was organised by Harro Schulze-Boysen, born in 1909 in Kiel. It was called the Rote Kapelle / Red Chapel. Schulze-Boysen was arrested and executed in Berlin-Plötzensee on 22 December 1942.

Germany's first democracy, the "Weimar" republic, was transformed into a dictatorship, ruling until May 1945, when the Allied Forces of France, Great Britain, Russia and the United States of America liberated Germany. The Bundesrepublik Deutschland / German Federal Republic (BRD) was established in the West while the East stayed under Russian rule and became the German Democratic Republic (DDR), a so called "socialist" regime under Russian control with the "Wall" separating the two German states.

Willy Brandt (SPD), announced, when he was elected chancellor in October 1969: "Wir wollen mehr Demokratie wagen" / "Let's dare to have more democracy". He introduced a new policy towards the East, "change through rapprochement", which ultimately led to the fall of the Berlin Wall in 1989, and the unification of East and West Germany in 1990.

Berlin became the capital of the new united German Federal Republic. Brandt was awarded the Nobel Peace Prize for his politics.

KIEL PARLIAMENT AND EXECUTIVE ADMINISTRATION

As of 1945, Germany's political constitution is threefold:

- The Federal Parliament and government in Berlin
- Regional Parliaments in the 16 German federal states ("Bundesländer")
- Parliaments and governments in each municipality

Today, the Bundesrepublik Deutschland is united again after the peaceful revolution of 1989, when the five eastern states joined the eleven western federal states.

ihs

City Hall

Kiel is a self-governing municipality. It has its own elected Parliament and lord mayor, and like every other German municipality, it has the power to raise taxes, such as business tax and real estate tax as every other German city. In 2018, Kiel's tax revenue was € 336 million.

Dr. Ulf Kämpfer of the Social Democratic Party (SPD) is lord mayor since 2014.

Kiel City Hall was erected between 1907–1911 from the plans of architect Hermann Billing in the art deco style, when Kiel was thought to have the potential to become a powerful naval force as Venice had once been. A 106-metre-high campanile was built, with a 67-metre viewing platform, accessible by elevator. Tickets for viewing the Kiel City Hall are available at the Kiel Tourist Information office.

Kiel Tourist Information
Stresemannplatz 1–3
24103 Kiel-City
✆ 0431 679100

A FEW FACTS ABOUT KIEL'S CLIMATE PROTECTION POLICY

Kiel, the capital of Schleswig-Holstein, is a very **green city**. Here, more than 60,000 trees grow, and the city has 133 natural monuments. These improve the air quality by filtering nitrogen oxides and fine dust pollution caused by road traffic, while producing oxygen. Kiel's air quality is good, which is not really surprising, given its location near the Baltic coast and its steady winds. There are exceptions to this, of course, on a few stretches of the hectic Theodor-Heuss-Ring. Therefore, in the autumn of 2020, Kiel installed air filtering machines from the company Purevento GmbH that clean the air of exhaust gases.

Incoming ships mooring at Ostsee- and Schwedenkai have access to **onshore power**, which means they do not need to keep their own engines running. This onshore power plant helps reduce climate gas emissions. The Port of Kiel magazine First Trade First Travel Issue No. 9, 2021 writes: "In future, the power will be produced by a photovoltaic system".

Kiel's sewage treatment plant in Bülk is fully powered by the use of renewable energy.

Kiel aims to be carbon-neutral by 2035. The city has planned a range of different measures to achieve this:

- The Stadtwerke Kiel AG, a municipal power supply company, of which 51 per cent is owned by MVV Energie, Mannheim, has replaced the former coal-fired plant with a **gas-fired plant**, the "Küstenkraftwerk K.I.E.L.". The new 20 gas engines produce 190 megawatts of electricity and 192 megawatts of heat.
- In the long run, even gas as a fossil fuel will have to be replaced by using **renewable energy resources** for power and heat generation.
- Today, 340 **photovoltaic modules** with an output of about 85,000 kilowatt hours electricity have been installed on the roof of the Stadtwerke canteen, reducing the Stadtwerke CO_2 output by 50 tons per year.
- The **Stadtwerke Kiel** were established in 1856, then named "Städtische Gasanstalt". Today the company employs 980 people and has a turnover of more than €500 million.
- In 1992, a 1,368-metre-long **heat supply tunnel** was built, which runs 38 metres deep under the fjord from

east to west, delivering district heat to 70,000 households.

Küstenkraftwerk Kiel
Managed by Stadtwerke Kiel AG
Hasselfelde 30
24149 Kiel-Neumühlen-Dietrichsdorf
✆ 0431 98793000

● In November 2022, Kiel Parliament decided to re-introduce a **tram system**. The old one had been given up in the Eighties, as in so many other cities. The new system will transport double the amount of people transported by the current public bus system and

District heat tunnel under Kiel fjord

Kiel's new combined power and district heat station

will run on renewable energy. It will take around ten years to bring into operation.

- Until then, Kiel will extend its bus routes with the aim to replace individual cars. The Kieler Verkehrsgesellschaft (KVG) is already using 67 **e-buses** and 33 **hybrid buses**, saving 5,000 tons of CO_2 per year. Altogether, there are today 200 Kiel buses in use. The use of diesel in these buses will be phased out in favour of renewables over the next ten years.

These electrical buses need to be plugged in every 70 to 80 kilometres, so the KVG has started to erect charging points at final stops, for example in Adalbertstrasse in the Wik, and in Suchsdorf with more to follow.

One of the electrical charging stations in Wik

A new initiative was presented on 28 August 2022, a so-called "climate bus", launched by Dr. Tobias Bayr of the GEOMAR Institute as well as Scientists for Future in cooperation with the Kieler Verkehrsgesellschaft. The bus is designed to make passengers aware that we are living in a climate crisis and need to reduce the use of carbon resources.

KVG was given the EBUS Award in 2022.

Kiel climate bus

- Public transport will also be extended by offering better and direct connections by power-driven ferry boats across Kiel fjord. The first **electric ferry** from Reventloubrücke to the mouth of the Schwentine river, is the "Düsternbrook" and started in May 2021. Its 78 battery cells deliver 819 kilowatts per hour power for a 10-hour run (lie F 2). It is the first electric ferry in a German seaport.

The hybrid ferry "Gaarden" (with 273 kilowatts per hour) will also provide public transport. Both routes will start once the necessary infrastructure, i.e. charging points at Kiel's main station and in Dietrichsdorf, is in place.

The "Friedrichsort" is the third electric boat crossing Kiel fjord, connecting both its shores and all those communities living in the area with the city by using the waterway, thus reducing noxious gas emissions.

• Schleswig-Holstein's first **greenhouse project** was initiated in the 1990s, a cooperative comprising 20 residential houses, a nursery, an energy centre, and a herbal sewage treatment facility. For more information, please contact:

ihs

Electric ferry "Düsternbrook", with Kiel flag

ihs

Electric ferry "Friedrichsort"

Ökosiedlung Kiel-Hassee, The Kieler Scholle Siedlungsgenossenschaft eG
Am Moorwiesengraben 22
24113 Kiel-Hassee

- Kiel offers all its public sector workers **bicycle use**. From the end of 2020 to 2022, grants have been available for employees to buy or rent bicycles that are used for commuting to work and travel to official appointments, following an agreement between the unions and the communal employer association (KAV).
- Additionally, from the beginning of May 2021, Kiel public sector employees will receive a **ticket** for the use of public transport on busses, railway and ferries. All these initiatives aim to reduce car use and consequently noxious gas and noise emissions.
- Kiel also has compulsory waste separation. Organic waste is collected and treated to produce **compost**.
- And over the bridge of the mouth of the river Schwentine, a **water power station** makes use of the different altitudes between river and fjord.

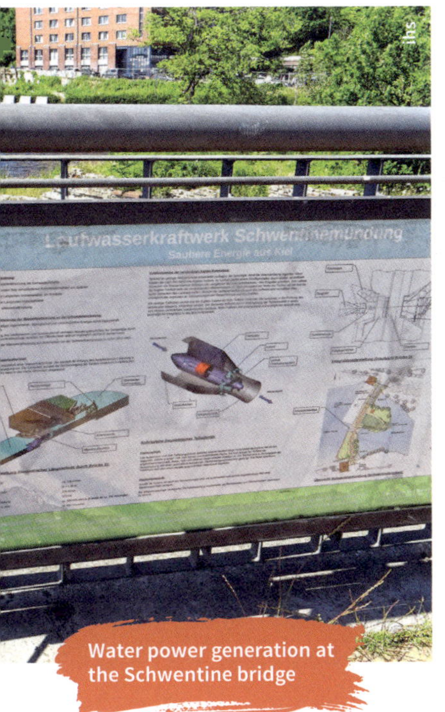
Water power generation at the Schwentine bridge

The city council is also strengthening its communication with local inhabitants to inform them about its policies and convince them that reducing climate emissions is necessary.

In recognition of these policies, Kiel won a sustainability award for German communities in 2021.

Seagull and doves: A seagull tries to shield her fish roll from doves

SCHLESWIG-HOLSTEIN PARLIAMENT AND GOVERNMENT

As the capital of the federal state of Schleswig-Holstein, Kiel is home to the “Schleswig-Holsteinische Landtag”/Parliament and government. The federal state of Schleswig-Holstein was established on 23 August 1946.

Former naval academy, today Schleswig-Holstein's Parliament

As of 2020, Schleswig-Holstein's population stands at 2.89 million.

Like all of Germany's 16 federal “Länder”, Schleswig-Holstein has its own codified constitution, as well as the power to raise taxes.

The 19th legislative term of the Schleswig-Holstein Parliament started in 2017 and will end in May 2023. There are 73 elected parliamentarians, 31.5 % of whom are women.

The Parliament is situated in the former naval academy, which was completely renovated and modernised in 2003/04.

The Landtag building is surrounded by the Ministries of Finance, Home and Economic + Traffic Affairs, with the "Haus der Kommunalen Selbstverwaltug"/House of Communal Self-Administration opposite in Reventlouallee.

Schleswig-Holsteinischer Landtag
Visits available
Düsternbrooker Weg 70
24105 Kiel-Düsternbrook
✆ 0431 9880

The inner courtyard is now a restaurant and has a glass covered roof

Schleswig-Holstein Parliament, modernised in 2004

SOME KEY DATA ABOUT KIEL'S POPULATION (2018)

Kiel's total population was 247,863 in 2020; 51 % are women and 49 % are male.

Kiel's age structure is:

Under 20	41,324
20 to 65	159,029
65 and older	47,203[2]

This age structure includes 36,663 students at four universities (2020), comprising 15 % of Kiel's population.

Employment (subjected to social security contributions): a total of 174,700 women and men are in employment, with 125,487 paying social security contributions (2020). In 2018, 60.2 % of Kiel inhabitants had a professional qualification, while 18.6 % had an academic degree. One of the reasons for the high proportion of qualified employed people is Kiel's status as the seat of the federal state Parliament and ministries, as well as its universities and city administration.

Number of employees in federal, state and municipal administration, including ministries, Parliament and universities, police, school and university staff, hospitals and judges 21,280

Municipal employees	5,322
Total public sector employees in Kiel	26,602

i.e. 21.5 % of all employed people were working for the public sector as of 2018.

ECONOMIC STRUCTURE

In 2020, Kiel's economic structure was made up of three sectors[3].

- **Primary sector**

Agriculture, forestry, fishery: 0.0 %.

There is one special product, grown in the fresh waters of Kiel fjord, the salmon trout, Kiel's **Lachsforelle**, sold on Kiel's open markets.

Kieler Lachsforelle
Salmon trout farm
Hasselfelde 40
24149 Kiel
✆ 0431 55698011
www.kieler-lachsforelle.de

2 A total of 247,546 inhabitants, according to Kiel "Quartalszahlen" IV/2021, published by Kiel Citizens' and Public Order Office, Statistics Department.

3 "Kiel in Numbers 2020", "Labour Market and Economy", p. 152.

Another seafood production company tried to grow mussels in the fjord waters. This was a good idea had it not been for the wild Eider ducks for whom the mussels proved easy pickings. So the **Kieler Meeresfarm**, founded in 2014, had to rethink their business model. Now it produces sea vegetables, such as sea kale.

Kieler Meeresfarm GmbH & Co. KG
Tiessenkai 10
24159 Kiel
✆ 0431 60833780
www.kieler-meeresfarm.de

Secondary sector
Manufacturing industry, energy and water supply, waste removal, construction: 16 %.

The latest Kiel start-up, this time run by craftsmen, is the **Strandfabrik** / beach factory in Friedrichsort. Here, long-unoccupied factory hall spaces can be hired for co-working, and products are manufactured, such as surfing boards, water tandems, portable saunas, seagrass products, upcycled furniture and cars, oyster mushrooms and much more.

Strandfabrik
Falckensteiner Str. 2
24159 Kiel
✆ 0160 95459567
www.strandfabrik.sh

Tertiary sector
Trade, traffic, hospitality, information and communication, finance and insurance, real estate, marketing, scientific services, public services, defence, social security, artisans, education, health services, social affairs, private household services: 84 %.

The data clearly show that the strength of Kiel's economy is in the service sector, as in every capital city. It also reflects the growing shift in all developed countries from industrial production to the production of services. Social scientists call this a "Strukturwandel" / structural shift, to be respected in all policies.

Here are a few of Kiel's key commercial enterprises:

	Jobs in 2021[4]
AWO, social services (3)	4,543
Caterpillar Motoren, mechanical engineering	750
Ferring, pharmaceutical products	430
Förde Sparkasse, banking (3)	1,300
German Naval Yards Kiel, shipbuilding	500
Hauptgenossenschaft Nord, agricultural trade (3)	750
IBAK, pipe inspection systems	350
KVP Pharma, part of the US company Elanco, vet products	800
Provinzial, insurance (3)	1.000
Raytheon Anschütz, ship building suppliers	580
Spiegelblank, cleaning (3)	2,100
Stadtwerke Kiel, power & heat generation	980
Süverkrüp, car trade (3)	950
ThyssenKrupp Marine Systems, shipbuilding	3,000
Vater-Gruppe, software (3)	500
Vossloh Locomotives, train engines	430

(The (3) indicates that these companies are in the tertiary sector.)

SHIPBUILDING (IN THE SECONDARY SECTOR)

Shipbuilding has a long tradition in Kiel. **ThyssenKrupp Marine Systems** is the important shipbuilding company in Kiel with sites in Flintbek, Emden and Hamburg. It has a 175-year history of naval engineering and employs a total of 3,600 marine experts.

Its subsidiary Altlas Elektronik, with offices in Bremen and Wedel, produces naval electronic system like hydro acoustics, sensor engineering and information technology for submarines and surface vessels.

ThyssenKrupp Marine Systems
Werftstrasse 112–114
24143 Kiel-Gaarden
✆ 0431 7000
www.thyssenkrupp-marinesystems.com

German Naval Yards was founded in 1938. Today, the shipbuilders offer a 391-metre-long pier and one of the biggest dry docks in Europe with a size of 426 x 38 metres, equipped with 60 cranes, one of them a portal crane measuring 110 metres in height and 163 metres in length with a 900-tonne lifting weight. Erected in 1975, it is the most prominent landmark on the east side of Kiel fjord.

4 According to the Kiel newspaper, KIELER NACHRICHTEN, study published 2 January 2021.

German Naval Yards
Werftstrasse 110
24143 Kiel-Gaarden
✆ 0431 239320
www.germannaval.com

There are many small shipbuilding companies, particularly in Friedrichs-ort-Pries, such as:

Gebrüder Friedrich GmbH & Co. KG
Founded in 1921
Prieser Strand 15 A
24159 Kiel-Pries
✆ 0431 394270
www.gfwerft.de

Rathje Yacht and Boat Shipyard
Founded in September 1922 by Paul Rathje
Prieser Strand 14 A
24159 Kiel-Pries
✆ 0431 2209 20
www.yachthafen-rathje.com

Yacht Service Kiel
Christianspries 30
24159 Kiel-Pries
✆ 0431 72972063
www.yacht-service-kiel.de

And North Germany's oldest sail manufacturer, founded in 1897, is in Wellingdorf:

Schultz-Segel GmbH
Langenkampweg 12
24148 Kiel
✆ 0431 723979
www.schultz-segel.de

Kiel's shipbuilding industry began more than one hundred years ago. The company Friedrich Krupp AG produced ships and submarines for the German Navy, with more civilian ships, as well as private luxury yachts, being built after World War II, as for example:

- The custom-designed **yacht "A"** for Russian billionaire Andrey Melnichenko, 143 metres long, laid down in 2005. The remarkable **Sea Cloud,** the world's oldest ocean seafarer, with a length of 96 metres, laid down in 1931.The tall ship **Sedov,** with a length of 117 metres, laid down in 1921 by the Friedrich Krupp Germania Werft for the Friedrich Adolf Vinnen shipping company of Bremen. Originally named "Magdalene Vinnen", it had to be handed over as part of the reparations to the Soviet Union in 1946. Today, it is used as a training ship for the University of Kaliningrad in Russia.
- Kiel is the home harbour of the German Navy training ship "Gorch Fock II", built in 1958 with a length of 89 metres. The first **Gorch Fock** was built in 1933 in Hamburg. It is named after a pseudonym of the German author Johann Wilhelm Kinau (1880–

The "Gorch Fock" returning to its home harbour after a full renovation on 4 October 2021

1916), whose most famous work was titled "Seefahrt ist not!"/"Navigare necesse est!".

Besides shipbuilding, Kiel is home to a range of **world-leading industrial production companies,** such as:

HELL Gravure Systems GmbH & Co. KG
Engraving systems for gravure form production
Philipp-Reiss-Weg 5
24148 Kiel
✆ 0431 23770
www.hell-gravure-systems.com

ihs

IBAK Helmut Hunger GmbH & Co. KG
Systems for sewer inspection and rehabilitation
Wehdenweg 122
24148 Kiel
✆ 0431 72700
www.ibak.de

Olfasense GmbH
Technological systems for odour laboratories
Fraunhoferstrasse 13
24118 Kiel
✆ 0431 220120
www.olfasense.com

Walterwerk Kiel GmbH & Co. KG
Baking equipment for waffle and snack manufacturers
Projensdorfer Strasse 324
24106 Kiel
✆ 0431 30580
www.walterwerk.com

Researchers from the Institute for the German Economy in Cologne examined the development of cities in addition to the level of general economic activity in their dynamic regional economic ranking in June 2022. They stated that "Kiel has (therefore) developed best. The port city has seen the best improvement in quality of life in recent years and has also impressed with its local commercial development."

KIEL CONNECTS TO TWIN CITIES

Kiel's twin cities post

ihs

Kiel has a lot of connections to other cities in different countries.

Kiel's twin cities are:

	Country	since
Brest	France	1964
Coventry	Great Britain	1967

On 14 November 1940, the British city of **Coventry**, situated in the West Midlands, was heavily bombed by the German Nazi air force, as it was the centre of the British motor industry. More than 4,000 buildings were destroyed. Coventry suffered more than any other British city.

In September 1947, Richard Howard, the Provost of Coventry Cathedral, visited Kiel and gave a cross made from medieval nails found in the ruins of Coventry Cathedral to the Nikolai Church as a memorial to the atrocities of war. Many other churches received a nail cross as well, for example the Dresden Frauenkirche and the Kaiser-Wilhelm-Memorial Church in Berlin. Today, there is a network of more than 200 orga-

ɔventry Cross nails (1947)

nisations in 45 countries sharing a commitment to peace, justice and reconciliation.

Then Coventry and Kiel established direct relations. Members of both city councils meet regularly, and a sports hall in Kiel's Gaarden district is named Coventry Hall:

Coventry Hall
Preetzer Strasse 117
24143 Kiel-Gaarden
✆ 0431 76865

The other twin towns are:

	Country	since
Vaasa	Finland	1967
Gdynia	Poland	1985
Tallinn	Estonia	1986
Kaliningrad	Russia	1992
Sovetsk	Russia	1992
Samsun	Turkey	2012
San Francisco	USA	2017

And there is even a city called **Kiel – New Holstein** in Wisconsin, USA with about 3,800 inhabitants (2018). Therefore, we can assume that north Germans from Schleswig-Holstein emigrated to the United States of America and took the name of their city with them, in the same way as people from Great Britain founded Boston and New York.

A delegation from Kiel's twin town San Francisco enjoying a boat trip, September 2017

SCIENCE AND RESEARCH

KIEL CONNECTS WITH DENMARK

Kiel has 16 grammar schools where pupils can take their university entrance examinations.

In the Federal Republic of Germany, Kiel is a leader in the field of integrated educational training in regional integrated professional education centres (Regionale Berufsbildungs Zentren – RBZ).

One of these centres, for business administration, was awarded the "Deutschen Schulpreis" of the Robert Bosch and the Heidhof Foundations in 2014 for its innovative concept which gives young people the opportunity to get professional training as well as higher education by attending university. Additionally, there is a regional integrated professional education centre for technology which participates in Erasmus programmes together with Halmstadt in Sweden, Vaasa in Finland and Gdynia in Poland.

RBZ Wirtschaft
Westring 444
24118 Kiel-Ravensberg
✆ 0431 1698400
www.rbz-wirtschaft-kiel.de

RBZ Technik
Geschwister-Scholl-Strasse 9
24143 Kiel-Garden
✆ 0431 1698600
www.rbz-technik.de

Kiel is a university city with a total of 36,663 students (2020, please compare chapter "A few important Data about Kiel's Population"), who make up round about 15 % of Kiel's population:

Universities:	**Number of students:**
Christian Albrecht University	27,477
University of Applied Sciences	7,824
University of Fine Arts and Design	548
Cooperative University of Applied Sciences	297

1) Christian Albrecht University (CAU) with the University Hospital of Schleswig-Holstein, was founded in 1665 by Duke Christian Albrecht of Schleswig-Holstein-Gottorf. The university motto is: "Pax optima rerum" / "Peace is the greatest good".

In the 18th and 19th century, Kiel was the second university city in Denmark after Copenhagen, and a centre for

German and Danish literature. Many important authors came to Kiel, such as Theodor Storm, Hans-Christian Andersen, Friedrich Gottlieb Klopstock, Johann Andreas Cramer, Jens Baggesen, Henrik Steffens, Adolf Schack von Staffeldt, visiting often.

And while the teaching professors were German, most of the students were from Denmark, as noted by Adelbert von Chamisso in 1834.[5]

Kiel's university practically forms a district of its own along both sides of Olshausenstrasse and offers the following faculties and courses: Agricultural Science and Archaeology[6], Economics and Politic Studies, Law, Mathematics and Physics, Medicine, Philosophy, Theology, Technical Studies, and Botany.

Christian Albrecht University (CAU)
Christian-Albrecht-Platz 4
24118 Kiel-Ravensberg
✆ 0431 88000
www.uni-kiel.de

The new **Botanical Garden** of the CAU is home to a 200-year-old herbarium. It contains 100,000 pages with plants discovered and collected by natural scientists such as Alexander von Humboldt, Adelbert von Chamisso, Georg Forster, Joseph Dalton Hooker and Eduard Pöpping during their worldwide expeditions in the 18th and 19th century. This ancient treasure is currently being restored and digitalised. The Botanical Institute receives con-

Part of the old university, built by Martin Gropius 1884, at Castle Garden

ihs

5 Heinrich Deterig, Andersen und Andere, Kleine dänisch-deutsche Kulturgeschichte Kiels, Boyens, 2005-
6 Here, the world's first professorship for history and archaeology was established in 1802.

stant queries from scientists around the world regarding genetic information on these plants. The collection will be available to view in the future.

For more information, please contact:

Professor Dr. Dietrich Ober,
herbarium@bot.uni-kiel.de

The new Botanical Garden of the CAU is home to the biggest plant in the world, the **Titanwurz** (titan arum, *Amorphophallus titanum*), originally from Sumatra. It only flowers every 10 to 15 years, and only for one day. It can grow to a height of three metres.

M. Nickol, Botanical Garden, CAU

Flowering titan arum

The **CAU Faculty of Engineering** is situated in Gaarden on the east bank of the fjord.

CAU's Faculty of Engineering
Kaiserstrasse 2
24143 Kiel-Gaarden
✆ 0431 8806001
www.tf.uni-kiel.de

2) Fachhochschule Kiel/University of Applied Sciences offers the following faculties and courses: Agriculture, Social Work and Health, Informatics and Electrotechnics, Mechanical Engineering, Economics, Media and Construction.

Fachhochschule Kiel
Sokratesplatz 1
24149 Kiel-Neumühlen-Dietrichsdorf
✆ 0431 210-0
www.fh-kiel.de

ihs

University of Applied Scien with solar panels at its fror

The old and the new building of Muthesius University

3) Muthesius Hochschule / University of Fine Arts and Design, founded in 1907, named after the architect Hermann Muthesius.

The university offers the following faculties and courses: Free Art, Art for Teachers, Industrial Design, Communication Design, Interior Design.

Students from Muthesius and the University of Applied Science have designed an autonomous electric ferry boat for crossing Kiel fjord and the Schlei fjord near Schleswig, north of Kiel. The new ferry, called “Wavelab”, has been built by the Kiel shipyard Gebrüder Friedrich and is 20.9 metres long, 8.1 metres wide, and only 1.2 metres deep. The steering technology is delivered by Raytheon Anschütz. The construction of the “Wavelab”, which was supported by the Federal Government of Germany, is one of Kiel's CAP-

The new building of the Muthesius University

ihs

TN (Clean Autonomous Public Transport Network) initiatives.

Muthesius Hochschule
Legienstrasse 35
24103 Kiel-Damperhof
✆ 0431 5198400
www.muthesius-kunsthochschule.de

4) Duale Hochschule Schleswig-Holstein / Schleswig-Holstein Cooperative University of Applied Sciences offers the following faculties and courses: Management of Business Administration and Business Informatics.

Duale Hochschule Schleswig-Holstein
Hans-Detlev-Prien-Strasse 10 and
Flintkampsredder 10
24106 Kiel-Wik
✆ 0431 3016126
www.dhsh.de

And to study at Kiel's **Volkshochschule** / Community College, employees can claim 5 days of paid further education leave per year.

Kiel Community College
Muhliusstrasse 29–31
24103 Kiel-Damperhof
✆ 0431 9015200
www.foerde-vhs.de

WORLD-RENOWNED RESEARCH INSTITUTES

Helmholtz Centre for Ocean Research / GEOMAR
Europe's largest marine and climate science institution (originally founded in 1870), employing more than 1,000 professional scientists
Wischhofstrasse 1–3
24148 Kiel-Wellingdorf
✆ 0431 6000
www.geomar.de

IfW Kiel Institute for the World Economy with the Leibniz Information Centre for Economics (ZBW)
The oldest of Germany's institutes for economics, founded 1914

The GEOMAR research vessel FS “ALKOR”, moored opposite Kiel Aquarium, Kiellinie, operating in the North and the Baltic Sea as well as in Kattegat and Skagerrak.

ihs

ihs

GEOMAR Institute

In 1996, sculptor Anatol Herzfeld installed twelve steel figures at the Geomar buildings at the mouth of the "Schwentine" river, calling them "Die Kybernetiker" / "The Cybernetics".

Kiellinie 66
24105 Kiel-Düsternbrook
✆ 0431 88141
www.ifw-kiel.de

Max-Rubner-Institut
Founded 1876
Hermann-Weigmann-Strasse 1
24103 Kiel-Damperhof
✆ 0431 6091
www.mri.bund.de

Kiel Science Park
Home to more than 100 companies with 1,600 employees, close to Kiel University
Fraunhofer Strasse 13
24118 Kiel-Ravensberg
✆ 0431 220866-0
www.wissenschaftspark-kiel.de

Bundeswehr Research Institute for Waterborne Sound and Geophysics
Klausdorfer Weg 2–24
24148 Kiel-Ellerbek / Wellingdorf
✆ 0431 6070

Maritimes Cluster Norddeutschland (MCN) e. V.
WTSH Wirtschaftsförderung und Technologietransfer Schleswig-Holstein GmbH
Lorentzendamm 24
24103 Kiel
✆ 0431 66666-868
www.maritimes-cluster.de

NOBEL PRIZE WINNERS WITH CONNECTIONS TO KIEL

- **Otto Diels*** (1876–1954), professor at Kiel University (CAU), awarded the Nobel Prize for Chemistry in 1950 together with his student **Kurt Alder*** for the so-called Diels-Alder reaction and the discovery and development of the diene synthesis.
- **Günter Blobel** (1936–2018), a Kiel student, awarded the Nobel Prize for Medicine in 1999 for his discovery that proteins have intrinsic signals that govern their transport and localisation in a cell.
- **Eduard Buchner*** (1860–1917), professor at Kiel University, awarded the Nobel Prize for Chemistry in 1907, known as the "father" of modern biochemistry for his discovery of cell-free fermentation.

ihs

Six (*) of Kiel's Nobel Prize winners are commemorated in bronze busts by the Schleswig-Holstein sculptor Jörg Plickat. The busts are exhibited in the Ratsdienergarten in the town centre

- **Gerhard Domagk** (1895–1964), a Kiel student, awarded the Nobel Prize for Medicine in 1939. He was forced to reject the award by the Nazi government. Dogmagk discovered that sulfonamides, the first kinds of antibiotics, counteracted blood-poisoning bacteria.
- **Walter Rudolf Hess** (1881–1973), a Kiel student, awarded the Nobel Prize for Medicine in 1949 for the mapping of brain areas involved in the control of organs together with the neurologist **Egas Moniz.**
- **Philip Lenard** (1862–1947), professor at Kiel University, awarded the Nobel Prize for Physics in 1905 for his work on cathode rays.
- **Wassily Leontief** (1905–1999), assistant at the Kiel Institute for the World Economy, awarded the Nobel Prize for Economics in 1973 for his input-output analyses and business cycle theory.
- **Otto Fritz Meyerhof*** (1884–1951), professor of physiology at Kiel University, awarded the Nobel Prize in 1922 for his work on muscle metabolism together with **Briton Archibald Vivian Hill**.
- **Theodor Mommsen*** (1817–1903), a student in Kiel, renowned 19th century historian, awarded the Nobel Prize for Literature in 1902.
- **Wolfgang Paul** (1913–1993), assistant at Kiel University, awarded the Nobel Prize for Physics in 1989, inventor of the ion trap, together with **Norman Foster Ramsey** and **Hans Georg Dehmelt.**
- **Max Planck*** (1858–1947), physicist, born in Kiel, professor at Kiel, awarded the Nobel Prize for Physics in 1919 as the originator of quantum theory.

INNOVATORS AND INVENTORS

Kiel has been home to many inventors and innovators, such as:

- **Hermann Anschütz-Kaempfe** (1872–1931), scientist and inventor of the **gyrocompass**, chart-plotter and autopilot, who later developed the spherical compass (his company has been incorporated into Raytheon Anschütz AG).

Hermann Anschütz asked Albert Einstein (1879–1955), a theoretical physicist and then professor in Berlin, to give his expert opinion on Anschütz's patent of the spherical

Hermann Anschütz and Albert Einstein sailing Kiel fjord

Landesarchiv Schleswig-Holstein, Kiel

compass. They became friends and sailed on Kiel fjord.

On 15 September 1920, Einstein gave a speech about his new Theory of Relativity and the relationship between mass and energy ($E = mc^2$) in Kiel's House of the Unions, the "Legienhof", as Kiel University did not have room for his speech. One rumour was that he was not invited to the university because of his religious beliefs, even though he was an agnostic humanist.

Einstein was awarded the Nobel Prize for Physics in 1921.

ihs

Einstein plate

Raytheon Anschütz AG
Zeyestrasse 16–24, 2
24106 Kiel-Wik
✆ 0431 30190
www.raytheon-anschuetz.com

- Engineer **Wilhelm Bauer** (1822–1875), inventor of the submarine, his model being named "Brandtaucher" in 1850, which the French novelist and utopian Jules Verne came to see in 1861 (today the Brandtaucher is on display in the Museum of Military History in Dresden).
- Physicist **Alexander Behm** (1880–1952), developer of the echo sounder, which took navigation to a new level.
- The neurologist **Hans Gerhard Creutzfeldt** (1885–1964) discovered Creutzfeld-Jakob disease**,** named after him.
- Surgeon **Friedrich von Esmarch** (1823–1908), director of Kiel's university hospital, who was responsible for many improvements in the care of wounded soldiers. In 1882, von Esmarch founded the "Deutsche Samariter Verein" / German Samaritans Association, precursor of the "Arbeiter-Samariter-Bund" / Workers' Samaritan Union. His second marriage was to Princess Henriette von Schleswig-Holstein, aunt of the later German Empress Auguste Viktoria. Kiel's Esmarchstrasse is named after him.
- **Walther Flemming** (1843–1905) discovered the lymphocyte formation in 1885.

- Physicist **Johannes Wilhelm Geiger** (1882–1945), inventor of the Geiger-Müller counter tube for measuring ionised radiation.
- The **Hagenuk Marinekommunikation (HMK)** company produces maritime radio communication technologies.

Hagenuk Telekom produced telephones for the German Bundespost from 1949 onwards, and from 1983 made the first cordless phone, the "Sinus", as well as satellite phones. The company was forced to file for insolvency in 1999 and closed in 2001 (originally situated at Westring, today the site of Kiel Science Park).

Hagenuk Marinekommunikation (HMK)
Wellseedamm 16A
24145 Kiel-Wellsee
✆ 0431 780350
www.hmk.atlas-elektronik.com

- Engineer **Rudolf Hell** (1901–2002), developer of the so-called "Hellschreiber", a forerunner of the fax machine. His company was merged with Linotype in 1990, becoming Linotype-Hell AG, and is today part of the company Heidelberger Druckmaschinen AG, a world leader in the print media industry.

Heidelberger Druckmaschinen AG
Doktor-Hell-Strasse
24107 Kiel-Suchsdorf
✆ 0431 3860
www.heidelberg.com

- **Gustav Adolf Neuber** (1850–1932) researched asepsis.
- **Prince Heinrich von Preußen** (1862–1929), brother of German Kaiser Wilhelm II and grandson of Britain's Queen Victoria, invented the windscreen wiper and patented it in Germany.
- **Heinrich Quincke** (1842–1922) developed the lumbar puncture.
- The gynaecologist **Prof. Dr. Kurt Semm** (1927–2003) from Kiel's university clinic created endoscopic instruments**,** paving the way for minimally invasive operations.
- **Prof. Ferdinand Tönnies** (1855–1934), resident of Niemannsweg 61 in Kiel, is called the "father" of Ger-

Memorial plate for Prof. Ferdinand Tönnies

man sociology (author of “Gemeinschaft und Gesellschaft” / “Community and Society”).

- The radiation detector sensor unit, developed by the team of Prof. Dr. Robert **Wimmer-Schweingruber** of the Institute of Experimental and Applied Physics at the Christian Albrecht University, was installed on the rover “Curiosity”, which landed on Mars 6 August 2012 and reported back that the radiation level on our neighbour planet is a hundred times higher than on Earth.
- And last not least **Hans Wöhlk** (1913–1991), he developed the first contact lenses in 1971.
- The famous **Kiel Blouse** or **Sailor Suit**, as shown by the two boys of the Hourticolon family, is a dark blue uniform introduced around the 1830s, a typical garment for young boys and girls. The three white stripes, introduced by sailors of the German Imperial Navy, were later copied by a German sports clothing company. Today, the sailor suit is even worn by girls in Japan and Hungary.
- Kiel’s first manufacturing company, a manufacturer of tin-glazed pottery, was established in 1764. The **Kieler Kunst-Keramik AG** was a historic successor to this tradition, re-established in 1924 on the initiative of city councillor Willy Hahn. Today, it is sadly no longer in existence, but their products have survived and are on display in the Warleberger Hof, Kiel’s city museum.

Hourticolon family (before World War I started)

Kunst-Keramik in the City Hall

dh

- **Kieler Sprotten**, small smoked sprats, were once produced in Ellerbek and became a world-known delicacy. At the end of the 19th century, there were 34 fish smokeries in Kiel. Initially packed in distinctive wooden boxes, the sprats were packed in tins from 1926. Kiel's last sprat facility closed in 1984. Today's "Kieler Sprotten" are made from chocolate.
- In 2002, after 20 years of research, the world's first **submarine with hydrogen fuel cell drive** was built in Kiel. Hydrogen fuel cells produce no noise or waste heat, and make stays on cruise liners even more comfortable, because they are vibration-free. From summer 2023, Europe's leading technology group, Thyssen-Krupp Marine Systems (TKMS), will start the production of Europe's latest fuel cells for ships and submarines. Today, TKMS offers the largest hydrogen filling station in north Germany.
- The world's oldest photo studio, established in 1843 by the **Renard family,** with a collection of more than 20,000 historic photos, including pictures of Kaiser Wilhelm II and his chancellor Otto von Bismarck, and the American president Theodore Roosevelt, dated 1910.

FAMOUS KIELER

Kiel has had two outstanding lord mayors. Both are honoured by city squares bearing their names:

- **Asmus Bremer** (1652–1720), was not only lord mayor but also a researcher of the city's history (author of the "Chronicon Kiliense tragicum-curiosum"). Together with his wife, he became the symbol of the yearly "Kieler Umschlag", an annual festival held at the end of February since 1431.
- **Andreas Gayk** (1893–1954), a Social Democrat, who invented the children's republic in Seekamp, and began re-building Kiel after World War II; for example, by planting small woods on top of the war debris.

More Kiel celebrities:

- The singer "**Alexandra**", born Doris Treitz (1942–1969), lived and studied for many years in Kiel. A square in the city of Ravensberg is named after her.
- **Klaus Borowski**, portrayed by the Kiel actor Axel Milberg in the detective series "Tatort", produced by NDR Television.
- **Klaus Groth** (1819–1899), a poet writing in Lower German and professor at Kiel University, his monument can be seen in the "Ratsdienergarten".
- **Nils Henkel,** the only three-star chef born in Kiel, guest chef at the 36th Schleswig-Holstein Gourmet Festival in 2022 (www.gourmetfestival.de).
- **Lotti Huber** (1912–1998), actress.
- The popular crooner **Sven Jenssen** (1934–2022).
- **Patrick von Kalckreuth** (1898–1970), painter.
- **Detlef von Liliencron** (1844–1909), lyric poet.
- **Johann Carl Gottfried Loewe** (1796–1869), singer, conductor and composer of 500 ballads, (the most famous is the "Erlkönig", based on a poem by Johann Wolfgang von Goethe), 17 oratories, six operas and two sinfonias. Loewe is called the "Schubert of North Germany", his body is buried in St. Nicholas Church in Kiel, his heart is depicted in a pillar of the Basilica of St. James the Apostle in Szczecin Cathedral, Poland.
- **Bernhard Minetti** (1905–1998), actor.
- **Friedrich Missfeldt** (1874–1969), painter.
- **Hans Olde** (1855–1917), painter and founder of North German Impressionism. He studied in Munich and Paris, returning to live at the Seekamp estate in 1892. He set up the Schleswig-Holstein Cooperative of Artists. In 1902, he became director of the Art Academy in Weimar, and in 1911 director of the Art Academy of Kassel.

Olde was one of the first to paint in the open landscape.

● **Theodor Olshausen** (1802–1869) was a politician and a member of the provisional government in Kiel during the German Revolution of 1848 as publisher of the "Kieler Correspondenzblatt". The aim was to separate the then dukedom of Schleswig and Holstein from the Danish monarchy. Threatened with arrest, he took refuge in the USA in 1851. There, he became editor and co-owner of the German speaking newspaper "Der Demokrat" (1856–1860) in St. Louis, Missouri, arguing for the abolition of slavery.

Poet
Klaus Groth

ihs

- His older brother **Justus** (1800–1882), an Orientalist, also supported independence from Denmark. In 1848, he became curator of Kiel University, but in 1852, when the movement lost its momentum, he had to give up all his positions. However, later on he became professor in Königsberg, Prussia, and from 1860 on, he was a full member of the Preussische Akademie der Wissenschaften / Prussian Academy of Science in Berlin.

Today the street where Kiel University is situated is named after the Olshausen brothers.

- **Raffael Rheinsberg** (1943–2016), sculptor.
- **Heinz Reincke** (1925–2011), actor.
- **Karl-Peter Röhl** (1890–1975), one of the famous "Bauhaus" artists.
- **Rudolf Schroeder** (1897–1965), an outstanding architect and construction director of Kiel city, designed the job centre building at Wilhelmplatz at the end of the 1920s (please compare chapter "A Selection of interesting Buildings & City Quarters"), and, in the 1950s, designed 21 "pavillon schools", with inside and outside rooms for each class. In 1952, the Kronsburg primary school designed by him was awarded the title of the most beautiful school in Europe.
- **Harro Schulze-Boysen** (1909–1942), born at Feldstrasse 68 in Kiel, a publicist and officer of the German Luftwaffe during World War II, then an antifascist resistance fighter, who was executed in Berlin at the age of 33. A pathway between Feldstrasse and Koldingstrasse is named after him.
- **Hans Söhnker** (1903–1981), actor.
- **Carl Friedrich von Weizsäcker** (1912–2007), born at Feldstrasse 68 in Kiel, was a physicist and philosopher.
- **Carl Zuckmayer** (1896–1977), writer and playwright, lived for a few years in Düsternbrooker Weg and founded the "Junger Kreis", a group of young actors who had the aim of renewing the theatres of the world, no less. In 1922 / 23, his production of "Eunuchus", a comedy by the Roman playwright Terence from the 2nd century BC, failed spectacularly, and Zuckmayer, naming Kiel city "Sprotten-Athen" / "Sprat Athens", was forced to leave in haste, as he described in his autobiography.
- It is also worth mentioning the famous initiative of 2007, the **Feinheimisch** network of producers and manufacturers, chefs and gastronomers, committed to offering only fresh, high-quality food made in Schleswig-Holstein.

FEINHEIMISCH Genuss aus Schleswig-Holstein e. V.
Am Wall 55
24103 Kiel-Vorstadt
✆ 0431 98654877
www.feinheimisch.de

7 Reminiscent of the German tongue twister: "Fischer's Fritze fischt frische Fische", translated as: "Fritz Fisher fishes fresh fish."

In Kiel, the Hotel Birke restaurant **Fischer's Fritze**[7] is a participant, specialising in fish and game.

Restaurant "Fischer's Fritze"
Martenshofweg 2–8
24109 Kiel
✆ 0431 5331311
www.hotel-birke.de

● Although this list is about famous people and human organisations, let's not forget our legendary stallion **METEOR** (1943–1966). With a total of 150 wins, he was the most successful and most famous jumper of his time.

In 1959, the sculptor Hans Kock (1920–2007) made a bronze statue of this horse. Today, it stands in front of the Staatskanzlei, the office of Schleswig-Holstein's prime minister.

"Meteor"

ihs

GREEN CONNECTS

Kiel is a very green city with lots of interconnected parks. This can be traced back to the city's 1922 development plan by city councillor Willy Hahn and landscape architect Leberecht Migge, which is alive and well one hundred years on. Their vision was to move the green rural landscape into the city and plant trees in every district for the recreation of Kiel inhabitants, for example around the "Hörn", the southernmost part of Kiel fjord.

ihs

Lord Mayor Andreas Gayk (1893–1954) took the initiative to plant 100,000 trees on the heaps of debris from the destroyed buildings in World War II.

While large parts of these plantations no longer exist, remnants can still be seen in a green space connecting the "Feldstrasse" with the "Koldingstrasse". It is called the **Little Gayk Forest**.

ON THE WEST SIDE OF KIEL FJORD

You can walk from the north to the south of Kiel through connected green spaces, designed by forward-thinking city planners, from Kiel "Schilksee" to "Pries" and "Holtenau".

- The **Kanalstrasse** in Holtenau district is the northernmost avenue of plane trees in Europe. The trees were a present from the Emperor of Japan to mark the opening of the Kiel Canal in 1895 and are now protected natural monuments.

After crossing the Kiel Canal, you can continue through:

- The woods of **Projensdorfer Gehölz** and **Wik**.

- The park **Forstbaumschule**, a former royal Danish forestry school (1785–1833) with a memorial stone to its director, Prof. August Chr. H. Niemann (1761–1832). It became a fruit tree nursery to provide Kiel's inhabitants with fresh fruit.

- The **Düsternbrooker Gehölz** with the "Krusenkoppel", an open-air arena with 2,000 seats, formerly owned by the farmer Heinrich Wilhelm Kruse (hence the name "Kruse sien Koppel" in Low German).

Barbeque in the Forstbaumschule park

WHILE FURTHER ON TO THE SOUTH THERE ARE

- The **Diederichsen** park named after Heinrich Diederichsen with the "Hirschfeld" viewing point, named after the famous German theorist of garden design, Christian Cay Lorenz Hirschfeld (author of "Theorie der Gartenkunst"/"Theory of Gardening").

- The **Old Botanical Garden** was originally established in 1669 as *hortus medicus*. At Schwanenweg, it opened in 1884, while Kiel's Botanical garden was relocated in 1985 to a new and larger situation near Kiel University.

  The Old Botanical Garden is still open to the public. It houses more than 280 different species with two small lakes and one of the biggest

Gingko trees in Schleswig-Holstein, as well as two huge primeval sequoias.

In 1891, a glass cupola was built at the top, from which amazing views all over Kiel fjord can be enjoyed. The room and a part of the park can be rented for private parties.

Old Botanical Garden
Schwanenweg 15
24105 Kiel-Düsternbrook
✆ 0431 568286
www.alter-botanischer-garten-kiel.de

● The large **Schrevenpark** with its lake, the “Schreventeich”, is connected to the west by a wooded avenue, the “Mittelstrasse”, leading to the University

“Kleiner Kiel” lake, part of the former surroundings of historic central Kiel

Top of the Old Botanical Garden

Clinic Hospital (UKSH) and the "Old Botanical Garden".

- The tree-lined road "Kaistrasse" leads all the way along the Kiel fjord from the **Ratsdienergarten** to Kiel Castle and on to the end of Kiel harbour, the "Hörn".
- The **New Botanical Garden** was built in 1985 in the Kiel University district and has about 120,000 visitors a year.
- Kiel **South Cemetery**, designed in 1869 in the form of a park by garden architect Wilhelm Benque.
- The **Moorteichwiese** connected to the **Waldwiese Park** and further on to the **Vieburger Gehölz** with the lakes "Schulensee", "Drachensee" and "Vorderer Russee" with a highly recommended walk along the "Eider" river from Eiderbrook to Ihlkate in Russee.

AND FURTHER ON TO THE WEST

- The **Hasseldieksdammer Gehölz**, **Hofholz** to the "**Ottendorfer Au**.

ON THE EAST SIDE OF KIEL FJORD

- The so-called **Förde-Wanderweg**, a 30-km-long walking trail starting at the Color Line Norway Terminal on the east side, connects Kiel with all the little villages on the Baltic Sea coast, up to the village Laboe.

- The mouth of the river **Schwentine**, a 68-kilometre-long river, flowing into Kiel fjord, its name comes from the Slavic word *Sventana*, meaning "holy".

Duck platform floating on river Schwentine

ihs

GREEN SPACES ON THE EAST SIDE

- **Wellsee** and **Elmschenhagen** cemeteries
- **Gehege Kronsburg** with "Kuckucksberg" hill (55.2 metres high)
- **Sophienhöhe** with the lakes "Langsee" and "Tröndelsee"
- **Brook**
- **Volkspark** in Gaarden
- **Schwanenseepark** and **Stadtrat Hahn Park**
- Kiel's **East cemetery**
- The **Dietrichsdorf cemetery** and the **Dietrichsdorfer Höhe**

KIEL IS ALSO KNOWN FOR ITS WILD ANIMAL ENCLOSURES

- **Hammer**, 15.2 hectares, small breed of sheep "Heidschnucken", Dexter cattle and deer,
- the **Hasseldieksdammer Gehölz**, 12.7 hectares, ox and bison,
- **Suchsdorf**, 3.6 hectares, highland cattle, fallow deer and mouflon,
- **Tannenberg**, 40 hectares, full of wild boars, mouflon and Damara goats,
- **Uhlenkrog** 2.7 hectares, with Soay sheep and white fallow deer and more.

LAKES

The city of Kiel has lots of lakes. The "Kleiner Kiel", the "Holstenfleet", and lakes in the Schrevenpark show a great variety.

We recommend taking a walk from "Schwanensee Park" and "Stadtrat-Hahn-Park" via **Tröndelsee** and further on to the **Langsee** in Ellerbek.

In Elmschenhagen, there is the **Wellsee**, in Hassee the **Drachensee**, and in Hammer the **Vordere Russee**, each one a leftover from the last Ice Age.

PORT OF KIEL

The Port of Kiel is one of Germany's main passenger ports. It connects Kiel …

Port of Kiel
Schwedenkai 1
24103 Kiel-Vorstadt
✆ 0431 98220
www.portofkiel.com

"Caledonia" took over the transport connection.

In 2019, Kiel welcomed 1.588 million **ferry passengers**:

from Norway	1.075 million
from Sweden	0.406 million
from Russia / Baltic	0.107 million

Port of Kiel building

… to the Baltic countries.

The first regular shipping route to Copenhagen / Denmark ran as early as 1780. Then, in 1819, the first steam ship

Cargo handled: 7.6 million tons (2021).
Scheduled ferry transport to and from (daily):

Sweden Pier (Stena Line) to the left, the Norwegian Pier (Color Line) to the right while a cruise liner is moored at Ostseekai in the middle

ihs

"Norwegenkai" ferries to Oslo / Norway

by Color Line GmbH

Max. depth: 9 m

Norwegenkai 1
24103 Kiel-Gaarden
✆ 0431 7300
www.colorline.de

"Ostuferhafen" ferries to Klaipeda / Lithuania

by DFDS Germany ApS & Co. KG

Ship berth no. 1, max. depth: 11.5 m

Ostuferhafen 15
24149 Kiel-Neumühlen-Dietrichsdorf
✆ 0431 20976444
www.dfds.com

ihs

The "Bahnhofsbrücke" opposite Kiel Main Station, starting point of the fjord ferries

The sloping building of the Schwedenkai / Sweden Termi

"Schwedenkai" ferries to Gothenburg / Sweden
by Stena Line GmbH & Co. KG
Max. depth: 9 m
Schwedenkai 1
24103 Kiel-Vorstadt
✆ 0180 6020100
www.stenaline.de

… and the direct connection from rail to ship (here to Sweden terminal).

Also, more and more **cruise liners** are stopping in Kiel with terminals in the middle of the city centre: In 2019, 803,061 cruise passengers started or ended their trips in Kiel.

Kiel is one of North Germany's leading passenger ports.

"Ostseekai"
Recently extended, ship berth no. 27 and 28, max. depth: 9.5 metres, opposite Kiel Castle, 300 metres from city centre
Ostseekai 1
24105 Kiel-Düsternbrook

By the way:

Today, electricity is delivered from land ("on-shore power"), so that ships do not need to leave their engines running. This helps to keep the air clean.

The newly built, enlarged cruise liner terminal "Ostseekai", built according to plans by eins:eins Hillenkamp & Roselius, Hamburg, and Ralf Dieter Ladwig, Bordesholm, was awarded for its design the "Bauherrnpreis 2021" in November 2021.

Flagge at Ostseekai (ihs)

Ostseekai Terminal for cruise ships (ihs)

"KIEL CANAL"

The Kiel Canal is like a "blue ribbon" running through the north of Germany. It is the busiest artificial waterway in the world, used by about 30,000 vessels a year, shortening the route from the Baltic countries to the North Sea, saving ships a 460-kilometre trip around the north of Denmark.

Kiel Canal is nearly 100 kilometres long (exactly 98.64 kilometres) and runs from Brunsbüttel / at the mouth of the river Elbe at the North Sea to Kiel at the Baltic Sea.

Its water level is at the same height as the oceans, separated from tides by locks in Brunsbüttel from the North Sea and the Baltic Sea in Kiel-Holtenau.

Built between 1887 and 1895, during the reigns of three German emperors, Wilhelm I (1871–1888), Friedrich III (1888), and Wilhelm II (1888–1918), Kiel Canal opened on 21 June 1895. Before, in the 18th century, there was a smaller canal connecting the Kiel fjord with the river Eider near Rendsburg, which flows into the North Sea near Tönning.

All the more, Kiel Canal has a further task, it drains 1,500 square kilometres of land in the river Eider region, into the North Sea.

Kiel Canal is managed by the Generaldirektion Wasserstrassen und Schifffahrt, a federal organisation, part of the German Federal Ministry of Transport, which is responsible for a total of 23,000 square kilometres of sea waterways and about 7,300 kilometres of inland waterways.

On a misty day through Kiel canal in keel line

ihs

Kiel locks
Schleuseninsel 2
24159 Kiel-Holtenau
✆ 0431 36030
www.wsa-kiel.wsv.de

Opposite the locks in Holtenau stands the **Old Holtenau Lighthouse** at Tiessenkai (International Registration No. C 1246). It is a navigation aid and memorial hall erected by the Kiel Canal Foundation on 3 June 1887. Above the main entrance is an image of two mermaids, representing the North Sea and the Baltic Sea, shaking hands. Its height is 20 metres. The old Holtenau lighthouse is part of the ensemble: Tiessenkai, Kanal Packhaus and the Holtenau Locks.

Crossing Kiel Canal by public transport: There is a small ferry boat for passengers and cyclists connecting both sides during daytime:

WSA ferry from Wik to Holtenau
People and bikes only
Wasserstrassen- und Schifffahrtsamt Kiel-Holtenau
Schleuseninsel 2
24159 Kiel-Holtenau
www.wsa-nord-ostsee-kanal.wsv.de

Holtenau locks

Old Holtenau lighthouse

Booking a Kiel Canal passage for leisure craft: To navigate Kiel Canal, please buy a ticket at the ticket machine in Kanalstrasse and follow the Traffic Regulations for Navigable Maritime Waterways. Travelling is only possible during daylight hours and in good visibility. This is important, as you will be sailing close to huge commercial vessels.

Recreational craft marina in Kiel Holtenau: There is a jetty available as a waiting area for overnight accommodation in accordance with canal transit.

The small canal ferry boat

REAL MOBILITY

High-speed rail, ferry boats crossing the fjord, buses in any direction—local, regional and beyond— and even a regional airport for private planes offer the best and easiest connections to and from Kiel.

The superfast ICE train at Kiel main station

MAIN RAILWAY STATION

The main railway station is situated in the city centre with the "Kaisertreppe" / "emperor staircase" originally built in 1895, modernised in 1999, with regional trains as well as superfast intercity ICE trains to Basel, Switzerland, Berlin, Frankfurt, Hamburg, Karlsruhe, Munich, Nuremberg, Prague, Czech

Kiel main railway station

“Umsteiger”, where cyclists can park their bike and switch to buses or trains

ihs

Republic and Stuttgart, please view www.bahn.de.

The “Umsteiger”/“connecting passengers” is the central bicycle parking and repair station at Sophienblatt.

Main railway station
Sophienbatt 25–27
24114 Kiel-Vorstadt

FERRY BOATS

There are two ferry boats: **Line 1 of the SFK** ferry runs to villages around the Kiel fjord up to Laboe at the north Baltic coast.

Line 2 of the SFK ferry goes from “Reventloubrücke” in the west to “Wellingdorf” and “Neumühlen” in the east, at the mouth of the Schwentine river.

Schlepp- und Fährgesellschaft Kiel (SFK)
Kaistrasse 51
24103 Kiel-Vorstadt
✆ 0431 5941260
www.sfk-kiel.de

ihs

Fjord ferry boat

CENTRAL BUS STATION (ZOB)

Located just across the main railway station, behind Hotel Atlantic, Auguste-Viktoria-Strasse, with a vehicle park. Buses run regional routes and routes to other German regions as well as Poland:

The Kielius
A regular public bus service to Hamburg airport
✆ 0431 666222
www.kielius-onlinebuchung.de

Vineta Verkehrsgesellschaft
Offers a more personal bus service to Hamburg Airport than the Kielius with the "KielExx"
Segeberger Landstrasse 2b
24145 Kiel-Wellsee
✆ 0431 7757575
www.vineta.net

INNER-CITY BUS NETWORK

Half of Kiel's inner-city buses run on electricity, with seven charging stations at final stops. For an overview of the network bus lines, please compare the last pages with the printed Kiel bus and ferryboat map or visit www.kvg-kiel.de .

AIRPORT

Kiel's airport has an annual capacity of 15,000 take-offs and landings in private general aviation and is very important to the regional economy.

The airport has undergone a transformation over recent years: the airpark and autonomous systems are modernised . According to "First Trade First Travel, Port of Kiel Magazine Issue 9/2021", in the northwestern part of the airport, two municipal business parks with an overall area of 100,000 square metres are being built.

Here's some technical information about the runways and the instrument landing system (ILS): tarmac 1,320 x 30 metres, grass 450 x 35 metres, ILS

ihs

Kiel's new central bus station / ZOB

Instrument Landing System CAT 1, Refuelling: JET A1, AVGAS.100LL.

Flughafen Kiel GmbH
Boelckestrasse 100
24159 Kiel-Holtenau
✆ 0431 3288243

CYCLE PATHS

Kiel not only offers lots of bicycle trails, but also paths exclusively for cycling, e-scooting and walking.

One of these is the 4-metre-wide cycle path from Kiel University in the north to Hassee train station in the south, connecting the Friedrich Junge School, businesses at Grasweg, and the Kiel Innovation and Technology Centre (KITZ).

There is a useful bicycle repair shop on the route, and no major roads to cross, making it a faster route than using a car, as well as being traffic jam-free and more climate-friendly, relaxed and safe.

"Kilia" sculpture and e-scooters, at Dänische Strasse

The "SprottenFlotte" bikes for hire at Kiel main station

ihs

SPROTTENFLOTTE

Quick-hire bikes from the company **Easily Rent Bikes**, sponsored by the Federal Ministry of Transport and Digital Infrastructure in Berlin. The scheme started in July 2019 with 17 stations. As of the end of December 2021, there were 65 stations offering electric bikes (pedelecs) and carrier cycles.

Easily rent bikes
Westring 284
24116 Kiel-Schreventeich
www.nextbike.de

CARSHARING

"Stattauto" and "car.los"
Lerchenstrasse 18–20
24103 Kiel-Vorstadt
✆ 0431 986460
www.info@stattauto-hl.de

TAXIS

Mare taxi Kiel GmbH
Lauenburger Strasse 32
24113 Kiel-Hassee
✆ 0431 77070
www.maretaxikiel.de

Taxi Kiel
✆ 0431 680101
www.taxikiel.de

CONSULATES

There are eight honorary consulates in Kiel, offering services when necessary:

Austrian Consulate
Bergstrasse 2
24103 Kiel-Brunswick
✆ 0431 552505
www.austria-kiel.de

Consulate of the Republic of Chile
Maklerstrasse 11
24159 Kiel-Wik
✆ 0431 3800909

Royal Danish Consulate
Lorentzendamm 28–30
24103 Kiel-Altstadt
✆ 0431 5921050

Consulate of the Republic of Estonia
Bergstrasse 2
24103 Kiel-Altstadt
✆ 0431 5194494

Consulate of the Republic of Finland
Wall 47–51
24103 Kiel-Altstadt
✆ 0431 981-0

Consulate of Indonesia
Brauner Berg 15
24159 Kiel
✆ 0431 394021

Consulate of the Republic of Italy
Wilhelmplatz 2a
24166 Kiel
✆ 0431 5700080

Royal Norwegian Consulate
Sophienblatt 100
24114 Kiel-Südfriedhof
✆ 0431 6640951

South African Consulate
Sophienblatt 11
24103 Kiel
✆ 0431 66386599

Danish Consultate

Götz Bormann, Royal Dansk Consulate, Kiel

SPORTS

Kiel is a city full of active sport enthusiasts. Its 200 sports clubs offer their 65,000 members (2018) a wide range of sports activities, such as:

AERIAL SPORTS

The "Luftsportverein Kiel" offers lessons in flying, jumping, gliding, parachuting and ballooning. You can even get a private flying licence here. To learn more, please contact:

Luftsportverein Kiel
Boelckestrasse 100
24159 Kiel-Holtenau
✆ 0431 323215
www.lsv-kiel.de

ALPINISM

Obviously, you can't do mountaineering in a location like Kiel. However, Kiel is home to a branch of the German "Alpenverein" (Alpine Club),

Ballooning in Kiel

established in 1893. It owns a mountain hut in Tyrol, Austria, at 2,800 metres altitude. 2,000 Kiel residents are members of the alpine club, regularly training in a climbing centre in Neumühlen-Dietrichsdorf.

DAV Sektion Kiel
Strohredder 17
24149 Kiel-Neumühlen-Dietrichsdorf
✆ 0431 5303149
www.dav-kiel.de

BADMINTON

Kieler Badminton Club von 1949 e. V.[8]
Feldstrasse 177
24105 Kiel-Düsternbrook
✆ 0431 805092
www.badminton-hotspots.de

BALLOONING (FROM NORDMARK SPORTFELD)

Airships, events & more
Thomas Oeding
Rendsburger Landstrasse 132
24113 Kiel-Hassee
✆ 0431 685473
www.balloon-sail.de

BATHING AND SWIMMING

Please compare:
www.kieler-baeder.de

OUTDOOR SWIMMING

- Beaches at **Schilksee and Friedrichsort** on the west and Hasselfeld on the east
- The **Eiderbad** in Hammer, an open-air pool, Eiderbrook, (✆ 0431 651653)

Swimming pool "Hörnbad" in Gaarden

8 The abbreviation e. V. stands for "eingetragener Verein" (registered association).

- **Katzheide open air-pool**
Von-der-Groeben-Strasse
✆ 0431 732423
- **Seebad Düsternbrook Lido**
Kiellinie 130
✆ 0431 34185
- **Seebadeanstalt Holtenau Lido**
Holtenauer Reede 30
✆ 0431 97997426

INDOOR SWIMMING

Hörnbad Gaarden
Anni-Wadle-Weg 1
24143 Kiel-Gaarden
✆ 0431 9011420

ihs

Schilksee
Drachenbahn 18
24159 Kiel-Schilksee
✆ 0431 9011460

University sports arena
Olshausenstrasse 70–74
24118 Kiel-Ravensberg
✆ 0431 8803736

BILLIARDS

Kieler Billard-Union e. V.
Holtenauer Strasse 279
24106 Kiel
✆ 0176 237 19 701
www.sportverband-kiel.de

CANOEING

Kieler Kanu-Klub (KKK)
Established 24 March 1921
Düsternbrooker Weg 46
24105 Kiel-Düsternbrook
✆ 0431 566002
www.kieler-kanu-klub.org

Kanu-Vereinigung Kiel von 1966 e. V. and Kayak club
Düsternbrooker Weg 44
24105 Kiel-Düsternbrook
✆ 0431 566674
www.kv-kiel.de

CHESS

Schachgesellschaft von 1884 e. V.
Holtenauer Strasse 181
24106 Kiel-Wik
✆ 0431 85075
www.schachverband-sh.de

DANCING / BALLET SCHOOL

There are 19 private dance studios in Kiel. If interested, please search for "Tanzstudios in Kiel" online. One public dance sports centre is:

Tanzen in Kiel e. V.
Suchskrug 1
24107 Kiel-Suchsdorf
✆ 0431 32903917
www.tanzen-in-kiel.de

"Serious flyfishing" in Kiel

DIVING

The "Tauchgruppe Kiel" is the oldest diving club in Schleswig-Holstein, established in 1954. Its hobby diver members can obtain the scuba diving certificate. The club supports the GEOMAR Institute's research into re-naturalising sea grass meadows in the Kiel fjord.

Tauchgruppe Kiel e. V.
Hinterm Deich 4
24161 Altenholz
✆ 0170 8310680
www.tauchgruppe-kiel.de

"Holstein Kiel" football stadium

DRAGON BOAT RACING

Organised by
Ellerbeker Turnvereinigung von 1886 e. V.
Grosse Ziegelstrasse 54
24148 Kiel
www.kielerdrachenboottage.de

FLYFISHING (IN KIEL)

Achim Stahl
Provides flyfishing lessons
Gablenzstrasse 6
24114 Kiel
✆ 0431 2202080
www.serious-flyfishing.de

FOOTBALL

The club "Holstein Kiel", nicknamed "The Storks" thanks to their red socks, was founded in 1900 and has more than 3,000 members. The team currently plays in Bundesliga 2.

Football stadium
Westring 501
24106 Kiel-Wik
✆ 0431 389024100
www.holstein-kiel.de

TEAM HANDBALL

The "Turnverein Hassee-Winterbek e. V." (THW), founded in 1904, is home to the famous “Zebras”, who play in the “Wunderino” arena. The “Zebras” have won 22 national handball titles.

THW Kiel Handball-Bundesliga
Ziegelteich 30
24103 Kiel-Vorstadt
✆ 0431 670390
www.thw-handball.de

ROWING

Erster Kieler Ruder-Club von 1862 e. V.
Düsternbrooker Weg 16
24105 Kiel-Düsternbrook
✆ 0431 577885
www.ekrc.de

THW handball team

HORSE RIDING

Kiel Renn- und Reitverein von 1902 e. V.
Olshausenstrasse 65–67
24118 Kiel-Ravensberg
✆ 0431 541644
www.krrv.de

Ruderclub Kieler Förde von 1985 e. V.
Elmschenhagener Allee 17
24146 Kiel-Elmschenhagen
✆ 0431 665374
www.ruderlobby.de

Rudergesellschaft Germania e.V, established 1862
Düsternbrooker Weg 42
24105 Kiel-Düsternbrook
✆ 0431 3207745
www.rggermaniakiel.com

FUN RUNS

Kiel has a well-known history for fun running. September 2022 will see Kiel's 34th fun run. Normally, about 10,000 people take part. There is a distance for everyone, from children and students to a half marathon of 21.1 kilometres. Temporary road closures are put in place for the runs. To attend, please contact:

ZIPPEL'S Läuferwelt Veranstaltungs GmbH
Fleethörn 25
24103 Kiel-Vorstadt
✆ 0431 16947271
www.zippels.de

SAILING

Kiel has a long history in sailing. In 1936, Kiel was the Olympic venue for sailing, and in 1972, the Olympic sailing competition took place in Schilksee.

Akademischer Segler-Verein in Kiel
Kiellinie 9
24105 Kiel-Düsternbrook
✆ 0431 561191
www.asv-kiel.de

Camp 24/7
With bathing in the fjord
Kiellinie
24105 Kiel-Düsternbrook
✆ 0431 2400070
www.camp24-7.de

SCB Segelclub Baltic e. V. von 1882
Kiellinie 64
24105 Kiel-Düsternbrook
✆ 0431 8058309
www.segelclub-baltic.de

Segler-Vereinigung Kiel e. V.
Kiellinie 215
24105 Kiel-Düsternbrook
✆ 0431 30034180
www.svk-kiel.de

TSC Traditional Sailing Charter
Tall ship sailing
Blücherbrücke 4
24105 Kiel-Düsternbrook
✆ 0431 23989904
www.t-s-c.de

University sailing centre
With 30 sailing and surfing teachers
at the "Olympia Hafen"
24159 Kiel-Schilksee
✆ 0431 3757811
www.segeln.uni-kiel.de

Kieler Yachtclub e. V.
Kiel Linie 70

24105 Kiel-Düsternbrook
✆ 0431 85021
www.kyc.de

KIEL SPORT BOAT BERTHS

The Kiel sport boat berths can be found in different parts of the city, such as Düsternbrook, Schilksee, Stickenhörn and Wik on the west side of Kiel fjord, and Wellingdorf and Dietrichsdorf on the east side (a total of 2,375 berths as of 2017).

KIEL INTERNATIONAL SAILING WEEK

Kiel International Sailing Week was first held on 13 July 1882. It is the world's biggest sailing competition with a parade of sailing ships, and about 4,000 yachtsmen participating from over 40 nations. Kiel International Sailing Week is held each year in the last week of June. From 2023 on, the 129th Kiel Week will celebrate its return to the Olympic stage. And the Olympic finals will once again take place on the fjord.

Kiel Marketing e. V.

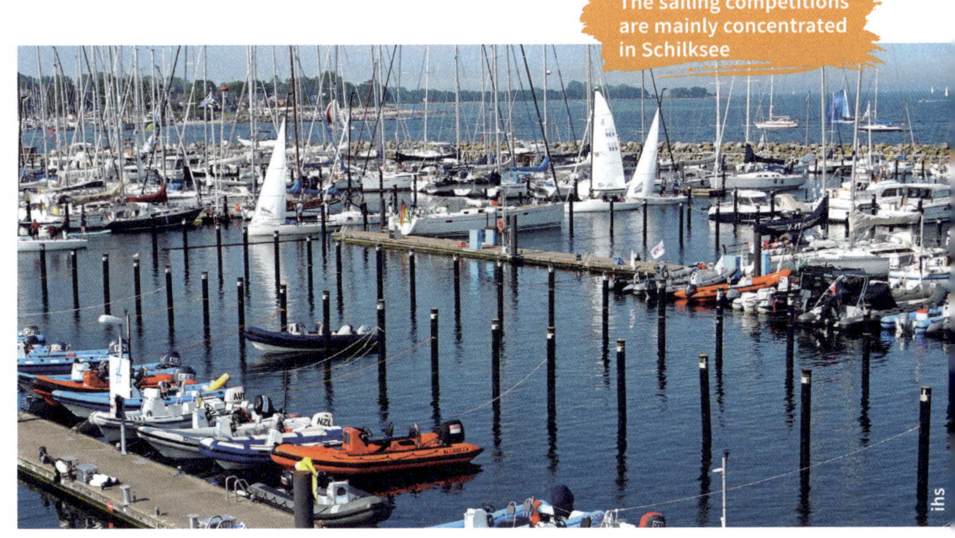

The sailing competitions are mainly concentrated in Schilksee

ihs

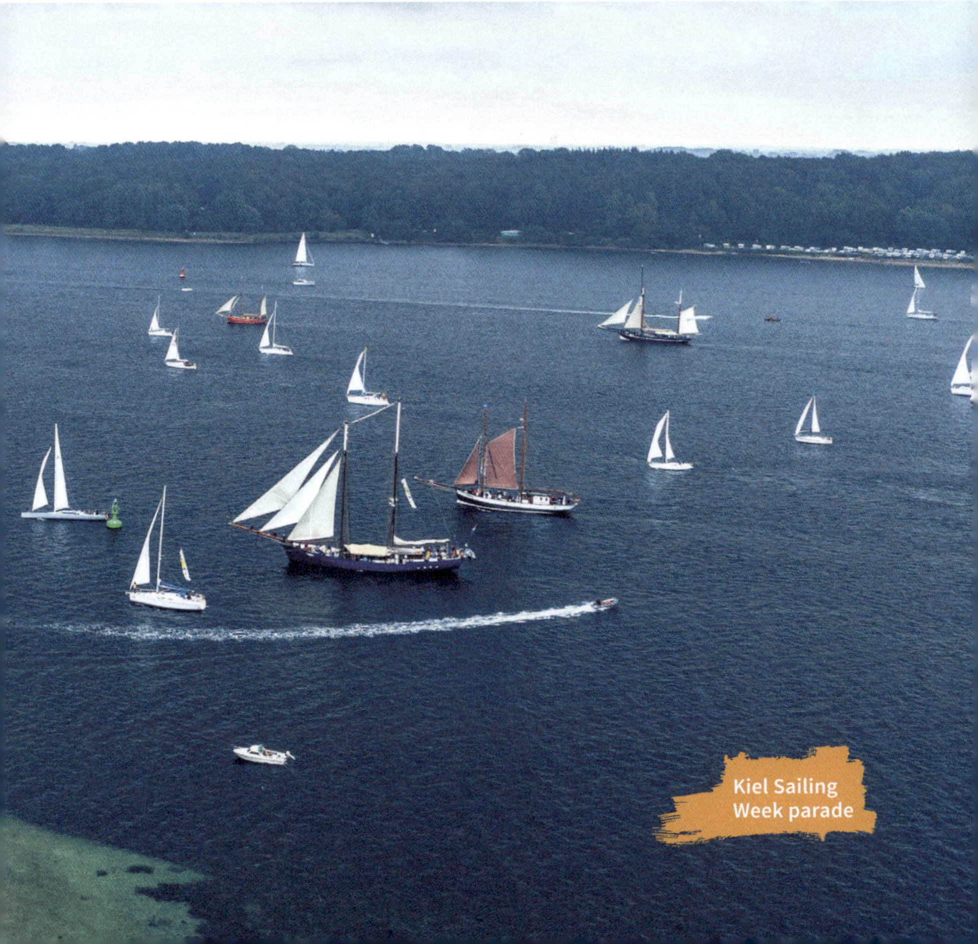

Kiel Sailing Week parade

People enjoying beach life on the other side of Schilksee beach

Feather hut

Building with the help of adults

And Kiel International Sailing Week is much more than just an international sporting event. It is also a folk festival, attracting about 3.5 million visitors from all over the world: www.kieler-woche.de.

There are even plenty of activities for children during Kiel Sailing Week. Jumping, a Punch & Judy theatre, and all kinds of hut building can be found in "Krusenkoppel" park, just opposite the Schleswig-Holstein Parliament building:

SQUASH

Squash Club e. V.
Göteborgring 83
24109 Kiel-Mettenhof
✆ 0431 53333-0
www.ksc-kiel.de

TENNIS

Tennisgesellschaft Düsternbrook e. V.
Karolinenweg 6
24105 Kiel-Düsternbrook
✆ 0431 85333
www.tgd-kiel.de

Tennis-Gesellschaft Ravensberg e. V.
Niebuhrstrasse 1
24105 Kiel-Ravensberg
✆ 0431 83847
www.tg-ravensberg.de

WALKING

Walking has a long tradition in Germany. The organisation "Wanderbewegung Kiel e. V." was founded in October 1972, more than 50 years ago. It is part of the "Norddeutsche Wanderverband" and the "Deutsche Wanderverband" with together more than 40,000 members. Regular walking tours and meetings are organised. For information about the next event, please contact:

Wanderbewegung Kiel
Mrs Susanne Fell
✆ 0431 2472354
or
Mrs Anette Cichy
✆ 0431 674223
www.wanderbewegung-kiel.de

COMMUNICATION CENTRES

Communication centres are a late invention of the 20th century, offering people food and entertainment at the same time. Some are even non-profit, such as:

Bunker-D
Dietrichsdorf Culture and Communication Centre by FH Kiel
Schwentinestrasse 11
24149 Kiel-Dietrichsdorf
✆ 0431 2101611

ihs

Dietrichsdorf communication centre "Bunker D"

"Pumpe"

Halle 400
An der Halle 400
24143 Kiel-Gaarden
✆ 0431 3640036
www.halle400-kiel.de

Max
With restaurant / bar
Eichhofstrasse 1
24116 Kiel-Schreveteich
✆ 0431 1229950
www.max-kiel.de

Pumpe
With art cinema and restaurant / bar
Hassstrasse 22
24103 Kiel-Altstadt
✆ 0431 2007643
www.diepumpe.de

Reparaturcafé Gaarden
A tech repair cafe
Elisabethstrasse 64
24143 Kiel-Gaarden
✆ 0431 9799534-0

Traumfabrik
With art cinema and restaurant / bar
Grasweg 19
24118 Kiel-Ravensberg
✆ 0431 54445-0
www.traumgmbh.de

Wunderino Arena
Entertainment arena for sports, music and exhibitions events
Kleiner Kuhberg
Europaplatz 1
24103 Kiel-Vorstadt
✆ 0431 98210-226
www.wunderino-arena.de

Wunderino Arena

THEATRES

Kielerinnen and Kieler also enjoy a lively cultural scene with lots of music and theatre events, supported by civic societies such as the "Gesellschaft der Freunde des Theaters in Kiel e. V." (www.theatergesellschaft-kiel.de), the "Musikfreunde e. V." (www.musikfreunde-kiel.de), the "Förderverein Konzertsaal am Kieler Schloss e. V." as well as the "Volksbühne Kiel e. V." (www.volksbuehne-kiel.de):

Kiel Opera House

ihs

OPERA HOUSE

Kiel's Opera House was built in 1907 by the architect Heinrich Seeling, destroyed in World War II and rebuilt in 1959. In summer, some operas are held in the open, for example in Anscharpark, on Blücherplatz, Ivenspark and Vinetaplatz, allowing everyone to enjoy the performances without having to buy tickets.

Rathausplatz 4
24103 Kiel-Vorstadt
✆ 0431 901-901
www.theater-kiel.de

PHILHARMONIC HALL

Konzertsaal am Kieler Schloss
The "Konzertsaal" close to the "Schloss" is renovated today, it has 1,300 seats, a restaurant und offers underground parking.
Dänische Strasse 44
24103 Kiel-Altstadt
✆ 0431 990710
www.kielerschloss.de

PLAYHOUSES

Junges Theater
A theatre for children and young people in the Werft park on the east bank of the fjord
Ostring 187 A
24143 Kiel-Gaarden
✆ 0431 9011200
www.theater-kiel.de

Die Komödianten
Wilhelminenstrasse 43
24103 Kiel-Damperhof
✆ 0431 553401
www.die-komoedianten.de

Niederdeutsche Bühne
For plays in Low German
Wilhelmplatz 2
24116 Kiel-Schreventeich
✆ 0431 17704
www.nbkiel.de

Schauspielhaus
With studio stage and bar
Holtenauer Strasse 103
24105 Kiel-Blücherplatz
✆ 0431 901-901
www.theater-kiel.de

Kiel Playhouse

ihs

KIEL MUSIC

Music is a language everybody understands, regardless of cultural differences. Music connects people. And people in Kiel are especially active in music.

CHOIRS

In Kiel, there are totally 24 choirs. A few of them are listed below. If you wish to attend, please visit the following website for further information: www.choere.de

Akademischer Chor der Uni Kiel
Founded by Klaus Volker Mader
www.uni-kiel.de/chor

Interkultureller Chor
Schützenwall 43
24114 Kiel-Südfriedhof
✆ 0431 2108181

Kieler Knabenchor
Förderverein "Kieler Knabenchor"
c/o Peter Priebs
Körnerstrasse 8
24103 Kiel
✆ 0174 1007858
www.kieler-knabenchor.de

Sankt Nikolai Chor
Alter Markt
24103 Kiel-Altstadt
✆ 0431 5578569
www.st-nikolai-kiel.de/sanktnikolaichor

Städtischer Chor Kiel e. V.
Rathausplatz 4
24103 Kiel-Vorstadt
✆ 0178 6051983
www.staedtischer-chor-kiel.de

JAZZ

Stadtgalerie
With cafe in the "Neues Rathaus" / new town hall
Andreas-Gayk-Strasse 31
24103 Kiel-Vorstadt
✆ 0431 9013400
www.foerderverein-stadtgalerie-kiel.de

Stadtgalerie (Jazz)

Pepe Lange

KIEL ORCHESTRAS

Förde Blasorchester
Eichkamp 4
24116 Kiel-Schreventeich
✆ 0431 675077
www.fbo-kiel.de

Kammerorchester der CAU-Universität
Max-Eyth-Strasse 15
24098 Kiel
✆ 0431 8803290
www.kammerorchester-cau.de

Musiculum
A non-profit workshop for children and young people
Stephan-Heinzel-Strasse 9
24103 Kiel-Vorstadt
✆ 0431 6668890
www.musiculum.de

Sven Sindt

Philharmonisches Orchester Kiel
Rathausplatz 4
24103 Kiel-Vorstadt
www.theater-kiel.de

Verein der Musikfreunde e. V. in Kiel
Koldingstrasse 25

24105 Kiel-Brunswik
✆ 0431 1490124
www.musikfreunde-kiel.de

MANUFACTURE AND REPAIR OF MUSICAL INSTRUMENTS

GUITARS

JTAR
Deichweg 20
24159 Kiel
✆ 0179 2385347
www.jtar.tech

Blaeser Atelier Lemke

Blaeseratelier Lemke

Stefan Zander
Königsweg 16
24104 Kiel
✆ 0431 676164
www.zandergitarren.de

PIANOS

Klavierwerkstatt
Dorfstrasse 13
24146 Kiel
✆ 0431 7890043
www.dieklavierwerkstatt.de

STRINGS

Geigenbau Albrecht
Knooper Weg 128
24105 Kiel
✆ 0431 5343427
www.geigenbau-albrecht.de

Geigenbau Tiedemann
Kleiner Kuhberg 38
24013 Kiel
✆ 0431 96073
www.geigenbau-tiedemann.de

WIND INSTRUMENTS

Bläser Atelier Jürgen Lemke
Eckernförder Strasse 93A
24116 Kiel
✆ 0431 2603636
www.blaeseratelier.de

LIBRARIES (PUBLIC)

Zentralbibliothek / Central library
There are ten public libraries in the following Kiel districts:
Elmschenhagen, Friedrichort, Gaarden, Holtenau, Mettenhof, Neumühlen-Dietrichsdorf, Suchsdorf, Schützenpark, Wik and Wellsee
Andreas-Gayk-Strasse 31
24103 Kiel-Vorstadt
✆ 0431 9013434
www.kiel.de

Schleswig-Holsteinische Landesbibliothek / State library
Wall 47–51
24103 Kiel-Altstadt
✆ 0431 69677-33
www.shlb.de

Stadtarchiv / Town Hall
24103 Kiel-Vorstadt
✆ 0431 901-3421
www.kiel.de

Universitätsbibliothek / University Library
Holds approx. 45,000 books and a Luther bible from 1522. Its oldest document dates from the 9th century
Leibnizstrasse 9
24118 Kiel-Ravensberg
✆ 0431 8804701
www.ub.uni-kiel.de

Bibliothek der Fachhochschule Kiel / Library of the University of Applied Sciences
Grenzstrasse 3
24149 Kiel-Neumühlen-Dietrichsdorf
✆ 0431 210 4800
www.fh-kiel/zentralbibliothek

Deutsche Zentralbibliothek für Wirtschaftswissenschaften (ZBW) / German National Library for Economics
Düsternbrooker Weg 120
24105 Kiel-Düsternbrook
✆ 0431 8814-0
www.uni-kiel.de/ifw

Bibliothek der Muthesius-Kunsthochschule / Library of the Muthesius University of Fine Arts and Design
Founded in 1907
Named after the architect Hermann Muthesius
Legienstrasse 35
24103 Kiel-Damperhof
✆ 0431 5198400
www.muthesius.de

ihs

Deutsche Zentralbibliothek für Wirtschaftswissenschaften / ZBW

A FEW SPECIAL RECOMMENDATIONS IN KIEL CITY CENTRE

ANTIQUARIAN

Antiquariat Schramm
Books, cards, maps and pictures
Dänische Strasse 26
24103 Kiel-Altstadt
✆ 0431 94367
www.antiquariat-schramm.de

ihs

Hoek & Hildebrandt

Antiques
Hoek & Hildebrandt
European historical artefacts, including glass, linen towels and ceramics
Knooper Weg 42
24103 Kiel-Altstadt
✆ 0151 20740145

BOOKS

Erichsen & Niehrenheim
Books in different languages
Dänische Strasse 8
24103 Kiel-Altstadt
✆ 0431 983050
www.bookservice.de

BOOKBINDER

Fritz Castagne Universitätsbuchbinder
Includes special paper works
Faulstrasse 20
24103 Kiel-Altstadt
✆ 0431 94647

University bookbinder Fritz Castagne

BEER (CRAFT)

lille Brauerei & Schankraum
The brewing and tasting experience of craft beer in the middle of Kiel city
Eichkamp 9c
24116 Kiel
✆ 0431 90889784
www.lillebraeu.de

CLASSICAL MUSIC AND JAZZ

Ruth König Klassik
CDs and DVDs
Dänische Strasse 7
24103 Kiel-Altstadt
✆ 0431 983050
www.ruth-koenig-klassik.de

COFFEE SHOPS / BARS

Café Fiedler
Possibly the best classical pastries in Kiel
Alter Markt
24103 Kiel
✆ 0431 26094455
www.cafe-fiedler.de

impuls
Coffee roaster and bar
Küterstrasse 7–9

Café Fiedler

24103 Kiel-Altstadt
✆ 0431 64084101
www.impuls-kaffeemanufaktur.de

Café Luna
At the bank of the Schwentine river
Schönberger Strasse 6
24148 Kiel-Wellingdorf
✆ 0431 21070665
www.lunacafe.de

Café and Restaurant Margaretental
The historic building high up overlooking Kiel Canal
Alte Chaussee 40
24107 Kiel-Suchsdorf
✆ 0431 12873705
www.margaretental.de

Café Luna

ihs

Restaurant Margaretental terrace overlooking Kiel Canal

Restez!
Boulangerie artisanale
24105 Kiel-Brunswik
Koldingstrasse 23
✆ 0431 23944922
www.restez.de

Werkstatt Café
Cafe and jeweller's
Dahlmannstrasse 11
24105 Kiel-Brunswik
✆ 0431 91865
www.werkstattcafe-kiel.de

CLASSIC SILVER CUTLERY

Robbe & Berking
Holtenauer Strasse 33
24105 Kiel-Brunswik
✆ 0431 9709252

DISCO

Die Schaubude
Trendy disco with various live music
Legienstrasse 40
24103 Kiel-Altstadt
✆ 0431 556600
www.kieler-schaubude.de

"Die Schaubude" disco

FASHION

Kelly's
Quality fashion for men
Dänische Strasse 24
24103 Kiel-Altstadt
✆ 0431 91560
www.kellys-kiel.de

Kelly's men's store

ihs

Stöhr
Quality designer fashion for women
Dänische Strasse 30
24103 Kiel-Altstadt
✆ 0431 94918

JEWELLERY

Goldschmiedepunkt Lorenzen und von Wenckstern
Specialists in remodelling pieces which are slightly out of fashion
Holtenauer Strasse 58 a
24105 Kiel-Brunswik
✆ 0431 565947
www.goldschmiedepunkt.de

MEDICINAL HERBS

Kräuter-Pflug
Herbs, teas and spices
Founded in 1919
Knooper Weg 46
24103 Kiel-Altstadt
✆ 0431 554476
www.kräuter-pflug.de

PORCELAIN

Abendroth Porzellan
Handmade in Kiel
Daniela Abendroth
Knooper Weg 109 (entrance from Jahnstrasse)
24116 Kiel
✆ 0173 9640633
www.abendroth-porzellan.de

SHOES

Kustom Kraft
Handmade shoes of the highest quality
Dennis Kieback
Rönner Weg 15
24146 Kiel-Elmschenhagen
✆ 0160 96438990
www.kustomkraft.de

ihs

Kräuter-Pflug

PRIVATE ART GALLERIES

Here is a list of Kiel's private art galleries:

Atelierhaus im Anscharpark
Heiligendammer Strasse 15
24106 Kiel-Wik
✆ 0431 30034027
www.atelierhaus-im-anscharpark.de
and
www.kunstverein-haus-8-anschar-park.de

Giotto Bente
Wood Sculptor
Wilhelmsplatz 8
24116 Kiel-Schreventeich
✆ 0431 566443
www.bildhauer-bente.de

Galerie Brennwald
Modern art and paintings
Hardenbergstrasse 20
24105 Kiel-Blücherplatz
✆ 0431 59677834
www.brennwald-galerie.de

Anschar exhibition "Dimension of Future" from 25th September to 30 October 2022 ("Until lions have their own historians, history will always glorify the hunt") with works by Thomas Kilpper (www.kilpper-projects.de)

Sculptor Giotto Bente

Galerie von Negelein
Classic antique furniture
Feldstrasse 70
24103 Kiel-Blücherplatz
✆ 0431 802140
www.galerievonnegelein.de

Punkt.um
bak Berufsverband Angewandte Kunst Schleswig-Holstein
Presenting ceramics and small wooden objects
Gneisenaustrasse 12
24105 Kiel-Blücherplatz
✆ 0160 5646870
www.bak-sh.de

ihs

Punkt.um: Exhibition “KERAMIK – 5 Positionen”

REGIONAL MARKETS AND FAIRS

Fresh food and flowers are produced in the region around Kiel and offered by their producers. The markets are listed here with their regular opening times.

Blücherplatz: Monday and Thursday mornings

Dietrichsdorf, Helmut-Hänsler-Platz: Saturday mornings

Elmenschenhagen, Andreas-Hofer-Platz: Tuesday and Saturday mornings

Exerzierplatz: Wednesday and Saturday mornings

Friedrichsort, Leuchtturmplatz: Saturday mornings

Gaarden, Vinetaplatz: Tuesday and Saturday mornings

Holtenau, Eckenerplatz**:** Friday afternoons

Mettenhof, Marktplatz: Friday mornings

Organic market, Asmus-Bremer-Platz: Every Friday

Schilksee, Funkstellenweg: Friday afternoon

Suchsdorf, An der Au: Friday mornings

Wik, Holtenauer Strasse /Elendsredder: Friday mornings

An **Antique and Flea Market** is held every first Sunday from May to October around the city hall.

A **Christmas Market** takes place every year around Andreas-Gayk-Platz and the city hall from the end of November to the end of December.

A **Fun Fair** for the whole family is held in spring and autumn at Wilhelmplatz. It has a Ferris wheel, swing carousel and much more.

Exer Market

ihs

KIEL MEDIA

Kiel is home to radio and TV stations, and has its own newspaper, the “Kieler Nachrichten”:

RADIO AND TV STATIONS

Norddeutscher Rundfunk
A public radio and TV
Schlossplatz 3
24103 Kiel-Altstadt
✆ 0431 9876-0
www.ndr.de

Offener Kanal Kiel
Hamburger Chaussee 36
24114 Kiel-Südfriedhof
✆ 0431 640040
www.oksh.de

“Kieler Nachrichten”

R.SH Radio Schleswig-Holstein
A private company, belonging to Regiocast, began broadcasting in 1986
Radio centre
Wittland 3
24109 Kiel-Hasseldieksdamm
✆ 0431 9869800
www.rsh.de

SAT1regional
Private
Kaistrasse 101
24114 Kiel-Südfriedhof
✆ 0431 3641200
www.sat1regional.de

KIEL NEWSPAPER

Kieler Nachrichten
Licensed in 1946 by the British Military Government, founded 1864 as KIELER ZEITUNG, also published in a digital version
Fleethörn 1–7
24103 Kiel-Vorstadt
✆ 0431 903-0
www.kn-online.de

A FEW SELECTED ACCOMMODATIONS

HOTELS

Atlantic Hotel
Opposite Kiel main station
Raiffeisenstrasse 2
24103 Kiel-Vorstadt
✆ 0431 37499-0
www.atlantic-hotels.de

Hotel Birke – Ringhotel
With restaurant "Fischer's Fritze" and inside pool
Marenshofweg 8
24109 Kiel-Hasseldieksdamm
✆ 0431 5331-0
www.hotel-birke.de

Lüneburg Haus – Restaurant and Apartments
Highly recommended for lunch in the middle of the old town
Dänische Strasse 22
24103 Kiel-Altstadt
✆ 0431 9826000
www.lueneburghaus.de

Romantik Hotel Kieler Kaufmann
With pool
Niemannsweg 102
24105 Kiel-Düsternbrook
✆ 0431 8811-0
www.kieler-kaufmann.de

YOUTH HOSTEL

Johannisstrasse 1
24143 Kiel-Gaarden
✆ 0431 731488

CARAVAN PARKING

Located close to Kiel Canal locks in Kiel-Wik

Caravan park close to Kiel locks

KIEL TOURIST INFORMATION

Tourist Information TI
Stresemann Platz 1–3
24103 Kiel-Vorstadt
✆ 0431 679100
www.kiel-sailing-city.de

City Sightseeing Kiel GmbH
Holstenbrücke 8–10
24103 Kiel-Vorstadt
✆ 0431 23942788
www.citysightseeing-kiel.de

Welcome Center / Tourist Information TI

Kiel **sightseeing walks** are offered from June to September. They last approximately 2 hours. Details are available from Kiel Tourist Information (details above).

There is also a hop-on/hop-off **Sightseeing Bus** from April to October (commentary in different languages) organised by:

Fördetörn / Harbour tours are offered every day in summer and last approximately 2 hours. For details, please contact Tourist Information TI.

Schwentine Fahrt / a motorboat trip up the idyllic “Schwentine” river is offered daily in summer, except on Mondays, from the “Alte Schwentinebrücke”

Sightseeing bus from main station

ihs

in Wellingdorf. For more information, please contact:

Hendrik Kühl
An der Holsatiamühle
24149 Kiel-Wellingdorf
✆ 0431 722428
www.schwentinetalfahrt.de

If you want to enjoy a trip on the ancient sailing ship **Hansekogge,** a rebuild of a ship originally from 1380, with a length of 23 metres, or if you want to charter the "Hansekogge" (in summer, the "Hansekogge" is moored behind the Schifffahrtsmuseum, please compare to chapter "Museums and the Museum Harbour"), please contact:

Förderverein Hansekogge Kiel e. V.
c/o Bernd Lesny
Radebrook 3
24147 Kiel-Elmschenhagen
www.hansekogge.de

A SELECTION OF INTERESTING BUILDINGS AND CITY DISTRICTS

Here is a selection of interesting buildings and city districts for tourists who have a particular interest in architecture and history:

TO THE EAST

The **Seefischmarkt**, today a commercial area with maritime as well as fish processing companies, was originally built as a shipyard. Up until the 1970s, it was the largest fish port and largest freshwater fish trading centre in Germany.

Krupp workers' housing estate in Gaarden, erected 1900 / 1901 in 24143 Kiel-Gaarden, (Blitzstrasse, Greifstrasse, Ostring and Preetzer Strasse).

The **Alte Mühle** / Old Mill, originally built in the 13th century, today a restaurant, is situated at the mouth of the Schwentine river, a 62-kilometre-long river running from the east to the west of Schleswig-Holstein.

The old **Schwentine Bridge** has been renovated a few years ago. A waterpower station generates electricity while the Schwentine's water flows

ihs

Krupp flats for workers

ihs

Old Mill at the mouth of the Schwentine river

down its wide mouth. A special ladder has been built to allow fishes passing the bridge upstream.

TO THE SOUTH

The remarkable **Hörn Campus** building. It hosts some office space and was built in 2000.

The **Hammer Settlement**, established in accordance with the planning of Leberecht Migge in the 1920s as a model for a self-sufficient lifestyle.

And last not least: the former restaurant **Felsenhalle**, originally erected in 1846.

If you want to have a look, it is recommended to walk up the Lindenweg from Königsweg. It is on top of a little hill and in desperate need of a litte TLC.

Felsenhalle
Königsweg 78 c
24114 Kiel-Südfriedhof

dp

Hörn Campus

The former "Felsenhalle" (ihs)

ihs

New residential district "Alte Feuerwache"

TO THE WEST

The **Alte Feuerwache** / Old Fire Station, a new built residential district between Dänische Strasse and Jensendamm in Altstadt, erected in 2016 by Böge Lindner K2 architects, Hamburg. It won the 2017 Polis Award for urban development.

The former **Arbeitsamt** / labour agency, today the Kiel Office for Social Services at Wilhelmplatz, Kiel-Schreventeich, built by Willy Hahn and Rudolf Schroeder in 1930.

ihs

The former Arbeitsamt, today the Office for Social Services

The **Kanalpackhaus** in Holtenau, an ensemble of historic buildings including the Tiessenkai, constructed at the end of the 17th century to accommodate the canal master of the former Eider Canal, is one of Holtenau's main landmarks.

The **housing estate around Schillstrasse** in Kiel-Ravensberg was built between 1926 and 1933 by the architect Walter Kelm (1883–1954) and named after the Prussian officer Ferdinand Baptista von Schill (1776–1809). Schill fought to defend the country against Napoleon's army. The estate features recessed balconies and wide inner courtyards. The houses are enriched with decorative elements by Alwin Blaue of the Kieler Kunst Keramik group, while the defining element of the "Wind God" sculpture is by Fritz Theilmann, Fichtestrasse No. 25.

Kanalpackhaus Holtenau

Schillstrasse

Industrie- und Handelskammer Schleswig-Holstein

Eckmannspeicher

The new **Industrie- und Handelskammer /** Chamber of Commerce was erected in 2004 by the architects Kauffmann Theilig & Partner.

The old water tower "Wasserturm Ravensberg", today renovated flats

Industrie- und Handelskammer
Bergstrasse 2
24103 Kiel-Brunswik
✆ 0431 51940
www.ihk-schleswig-holstein.de

The **Eckmannspeicher** a listed building and former granary, near STENA LINE, at Kaistrasse 33, erected in the 1920s by the architect Ernst Stoffers and operated until the 1970s. It was renovated in 2011, and is now used for the harbour terminal.

The **Old Water Tower** in Kiel-Ravensberg served as a water supply system in 1896 by Rudolph Schmidt. It is situated at the highest part of the Ravensberg. With a height of 34 metres, it was taken out of order in 1990 and is now a residential building: Niebuhrstrasse 5.

The new Holstenfleet

ihs

Bootshafen and **Holstenfleet** connect the districts Altstadt and Vorstadt with the "Kleine Kiel" lake surrounding the historic centre of Kiel.

The new Holstenfleet has been remodelled according to the former water ring around the old town. It was awarded a prize for urban public space design by the "Bund Deutscher Landschaftsarchitekten" and as well with the "Deutsche Ingenieurpreis Strasse und Verkehr" 2021.

Alter Markt is the historic market place in the old part of the city. Today it is a space for rest and relaxation with restaurants and coffee shops.

TO THE NORTH

The **Olympic Centre** Kiel-Schilksee was purposely built for the Olympic Games sailing competition in 1972 by the architects Hinrich Storch and Walter Ehlers.

"Alter Markt"

A FEW SUGGESTIONS FOR A DAY OUT (OR A FEW HOURS) WITH A YOUNG FAMILY

The **Katholikenwiese,** Kiel's largest children's playground, is located in the park Forstbaumschule. From Kiel centre, take bus No. 32 in the direction of "Wik" (15 minutes) and leave at "Yorkstrasse". Then walk a few yards into the same direction, until you see Kiel's largest playground, the "Katholikenwiese", to the right, close to St. Heinrich Church (Catholic).

The playground is part of **Forstbaumschule** park, leading down to Kiel fjord. It is as well the name of one

The huge Katholikenwiese playground

Restaurant Forstbaumschule

of Kiel's most frequented cafe-restaurants, where live music is played on most weekends.

The **Aquarium GEOMAR,** Kiellinie, is situated at bus stop "Schwanenweg", close to the fjord. It presents lots of marine animals, such as herrings and seals.

Then further on to the north, take a stroll on "Kiellinie", leave the fjord to your right and you will find lots of interesting cafes and restaurants to your left.

GEOMAR Aquarium

Düsternbrooker Weg 20 / entrance from "Kiellinie"
24105 Kiel-Düsternbrook
✆ 0431 6001637
www.aquarium-kiel.de

Herrings in Kiel Aquarium

Walking along the "Kiellinie" on a sunny Sunday

dh

Walk further on and there is the **Seebar** to your right, an outdoor swimming experience in the fjord with a restaurant built on a wooden pier.

Seebar
Kiellinie 130
24105 Kiel-Düsternbrook
✆ 0431 34185
www.seebad-duesternbrook.de

Another chance for children to spend time in free play is the **Kinder- und Jugendbauernhof** / "Young People's City Farm" in Mettenhof, organised by the AWO Arbeiterwohlfahrt Kiel e.V., based on a Danish model. Here, children can learn how to build and to grow food. It is a rather unique example for Schleswig-Holstein, showing that playing means development, that it supports health, and builds children's personalities:

Kinder- und Jugendbauernhof
Jens Lankuttis
Skandinaviendamm 250
24109 Kiel-Mettenhof
✆ 0431 520322
www.awo-kiel.de

For an unforgettable experience with a high climbing challenge, the "high spirits course", visit **Falckensteiner Strand**. From Kiel centre, take bus No. 91 in the direction of Friedrichsort (approx. 50 minutes) and leave at stop "An der Schanze", walk a few yards to No 44a, where you will discover one of Kiel's best ice cafes, "Neitsch".

Then follow the road Brauner Berg (there is a Chinese restaurant on your right) for about one hundred yards and you will arrive at Kiel's highest climbing challenge, the **Hochseilgarten** / high ropes course:

The "Hochseilgarten" is close to "Falckensteiner Strand", a beautiful spot to view the "Friedrichsort" lighthouse and to dip into the water, watching ships pass by as they move towards Kiel Canal.

Along the walkway to the north, there is a variety of cafes and restaurants to choose from.

Falckensteiner Strand 15
24159 Kiel-Holtenau
✆ 0431 3104947
www.hochseilgarten-kiel.de

“Hochseilgarten”

ihs

EPILOGUE

Dear Reader,

this walk through Kiel provided a great overview of the city's past and present. It showed that the capital of Schleswig-Holstein is a city of tradition and of trendsetting developments. Key drivers of the future will be – as always – economy and science. Kiel calls itself "City of marine protection". It is already one of the leading places in Germany and Europe in marine research and marine production. And the future will provide even more possibilities in this field.

However, for the further development of Kiel, we need vital urban districts, innovative science-campuses and – of course – highly productive industrial estates. A huge chance is emerging in the North of Kiel, North of the Kiel Canal: in Friedrichsort, Pries and Holtenau areas are reconstructed and thus revitalised. In the next five to ten years the industrial estate Friedrichsort will be completely restructured, Holtenau-Ost (MFG 5), formerly used by the military, will be turned into an urban district for work, living and leisure, and the area around the airport will be evolved with a focus on high-technology companies. These developments will set new standards and will generate new economic impulses for the whole region.

In the opposite direction – the South of Kiel – another urban district will be developed within the next years. New living space is created for families and workers and new space will be available for companies. This area is next to one of the biggest industrial estates in Schleswig-Holstein: Wellsee. So, new chances will also arise in the South of Kiel.

Important for all these areas, as well as the Seefischmarkt in the East and the city centre in the West, is a good transport infrastructure. Kiel will go new ways with the development of a new public transport system and the further improvement of cycle paths and high quality pedestrian areas. But that is just one side. The extension of the motorway in the South, the steady improvement of the railway connection, the intense works at the Kiel Canal and the good quality of the regional airport create an accessibility that is quite unique – in Germany!

When we really focus on the development of the industrial estates and the new urban districts, when we really sustainably improve the transport infrastructure and when we also create an environment for productivity, creativity, science and technology transfer, then Kiel will be a highly attractive place for people of all ages for living, working, learning and more. We will keep the positive power in the North and will further expand it.

As interesting as a walk through Kiel is nowadays – it will be increasingly interesting in the future!

Knud Hansen
President
Chamber of Commerce and
Industry Kiel

IHK

IHK President Hansen

ACKNOWLEDGEMENTS

While we want to thank Kielerinnen and Kielers for all their interesting information offered which is included in this publication, there are a few men whom we would like to thank especially, i.e. Dr. Klaus Alberts, Dr. Dieter Hartwig, Jens Jacobus, Maren und Dr. Jürgen Jensen, Dr. Dirk Claus, Dr. Jörn Biel, Jörn Genoux, Dr. Martin Kruse and Dr. Ekkehard Wienholtz. Without them, their knowledge, expertise and engagement for our lively city of Kiel, the most northern of todays sixteen Bundesländer in Germany, our guide would have been less interesting. We hope they enjoyed working with us as much as we did.

Furthermore we thank Sharon Howe for her support with writing in English and Yvette Bartholomew for her technical support. If there are still errors found, they are the only responsibility of the author.

PHOTO CREDITS

Pictures are of different origins:
Bläser Atelier Lemke, Dänisches Konsulat, Holstein Kiel (football), photojournalist Dirk Hourticolon (dh), Industrie- und Handelskammer, Kiel Marketing e.V., Kieler Stadtwerke AG, Kieler Verkehrsgesellschaft mbH (KVG), Dr. Martin Nickol/CAU, Thomas Oeding, Philharmonisches Orchester, Schleswig-Holsteinisches Landesarchiv, Stadt Kiel, Stadtarchiv, St. Nikolai Chor, THW (team handball), and Dr. Irene Schöne (ihs).

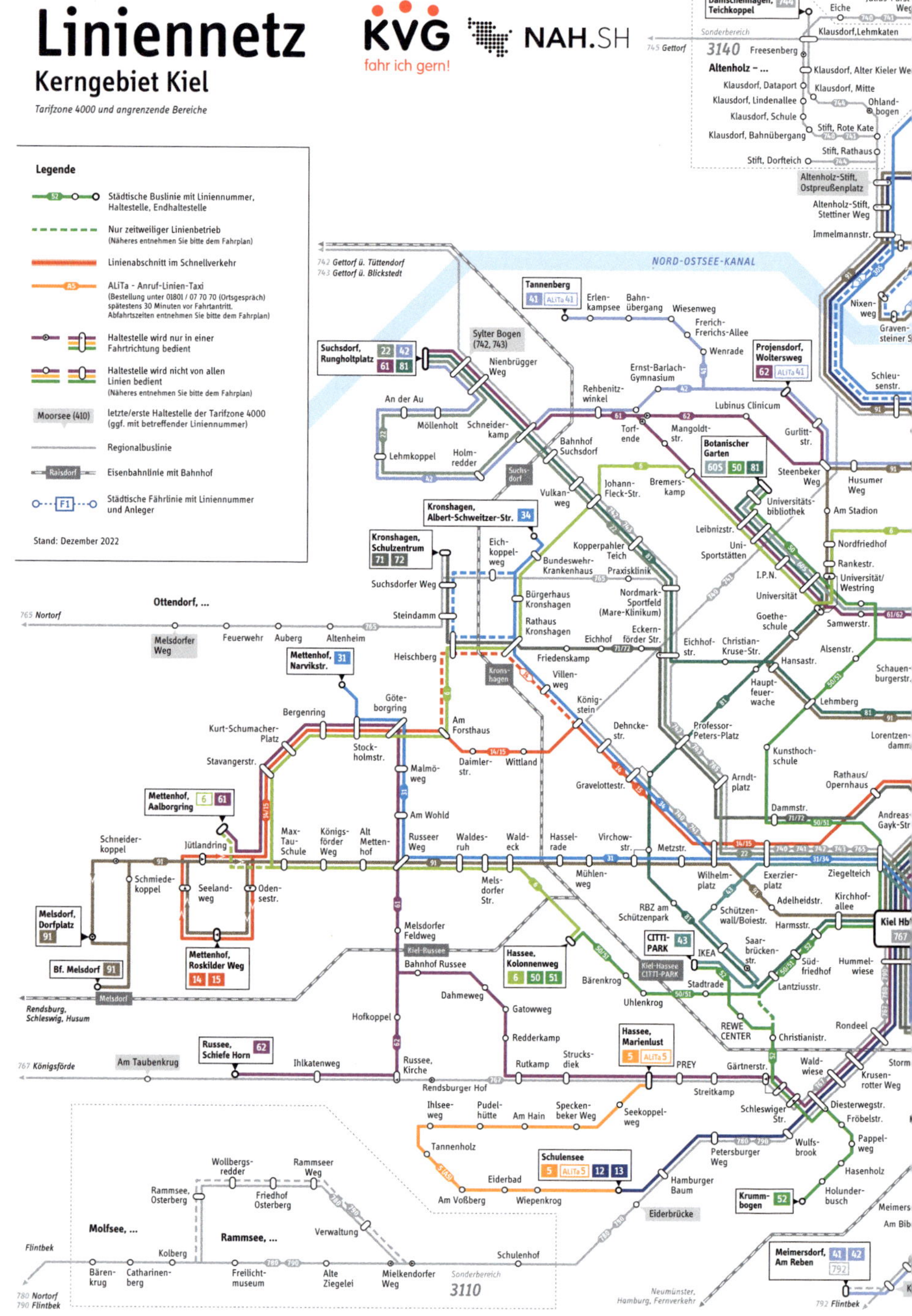
Liniennetz
Kerngebiet Kiel
Tarifzone 4000 und angrenzende Bereiche
KVG
fahr ich gern!
NAH.SH
Legende
Städtische Buslinie mit Liniennummer, Haltestelle, Endhaltestelle
Nur zeitweiliger Linienbetrieb (Näheres entnehmen Sie bitte dem Fahrplan)
Linienabschnitt im Schnellverkehr
ALiTa - Anruf-Linien-Taxi (Bestellung unter 01801 / 07 70 70 (Ortsgespräch) spätestens 30 Minuten vor Fahrtantritt. Abfahrtszeiten entnehmen Sie bitte dem Fahrplan)
Haltestelle wird nur in einer Fahrtrichtung bedient
Haltestelle wird nicht von allen Linien bedient (Näheres entnehmen Sie bitte dem Fahrplan)
Moorsee (410)
letzte/erste Haltestelle der Tarifzone 4000 (ggf. mit betreffender Liniennummer)
Regionalbuslinie
Raisdorf
Eisenbahnlinie mit Bahnhof
Städtische Fährlinie mit Liniennummer und Anleger
Stand: Dezember 2022
Dänischenhagen, Teichkoppel
Eiche
Julius-Fürst-Weg
Sonderbereich
3140
Klausdorf, Lehmkaten
745 Gettorf
Freesenberg
Altenholz – ...
Klausdorf, Alter Kieler Weg
Klausdorf, Dataport
Klausdorf, Mitte
Klausdorf, Lindenallee
Ohlandbogen
Klausdorf, Schule
Stift, Rote Kate
Klausdorf, Bahnübergang
Stift, Rathaus
Stift, Dorfteich
Altenholz-Stift, Ostpreußenplatz
Altenholz-Stift, Stettiner Weg
Immelmannstr.
NORD-OSTSEE-KANAL
742 Gettorf ü. Tüttendorf
743 Gettorf ü. Blickstedt
Tannenberg
Erlenkampsee
Bahnübergang
Wiesenweg
Frerich-Frerichs-Allee
Wenrade
Projensdorf, Woltersweg
Nixenweg
Gravensteiner Str.
Schleusenstr.
Suchsdorf, Rungholtplatz
Sylter Bogen (742, 743)
Nienbrügger Weg
Ernst-Barlach-Gymnasium
Rehbenitzwinkel
An der Au
Möllenholt
Schneiderkamp
Lubinus Clinicum
Torfende
Mangoldtstr.
Gurlittstr.
Lehmkoppel
Holmredder
Bahnhof Suchsdorf
Botanischer Garten
Steenbeker Weg
Husumer Weg
Suchsdorf
Vulkanweg
Johann-Fleck-Str.
Bremerskamp
Universitätsbibliothek
Am Stadion
Kronshagen, Albert-Schweitzer-Str.
Leibnizstr.
Kronshagen, Schulzentrum
Eichkoppelweg
Kopperpahler Teich
Uni-Sportstätten
Nordfriedhof
Bundeswehr-Krankenhaus
Praxisklinik
Rankestr.
Suchsdorfer Weg
I.P.N.
Universität/Westring
Ottendorf, ...
765 Nortorf
Bürgerhaus Kronshagen
Nordmark-Sportfeld (Mare-Klinikum)
Universität
Steindamm
Goetheschule
Samwerstr.
Melsdorfer Weg
Feuerwehr
Auberg
Altenheim
Rathaus Kronshagen
Eckernförder Str.
Eichhof
Eichhofstr.
Christian-Kruse-Str.
Alsenstr.
Mettenhof, Narvikstr.
Heischberg
Friedenskamp
Kronshagen
Hansastr.
Schauenburgerstr.
Villenweg
Hauptfeuerwache
Lehmberg
Götebor gring
Königstein
Bergenring
Am Forsthaus
Dehnckestr.
Professor-Peters-Platz
Lorentzendamm
Kurt-Schumacher-Platz
Kunsthochschule
Stockholmstr.
Daimlerstr.
Wittland
Rathaus/Opernhaus
Stavangerstr.
Malmöweg
Arndtplatz
Gravelottestr.
Dammstr.
Mettenhof, Aalborgring
Am Wohld
Andreas-Gayk-Str.
Schneiderkoppel
Jütlandring
Max-Tau-Schule
Königsförder Weg
Alt Mettenhof
Russeer Weg
Waldesruh
Waldeck
Hasselrade
Virchowstr.
Metzstr.
Schmiedekoppel
Seelandweg
Odensestr.
Mühlenweg
Melsdorfer Str.
Wilhelmplatz
Exerzierplatz
Ziegelteich
Adelheidstr.
Kirchhofallee
Melsdorf, Dorfplatz
Schützenwall/Boiestr.
RBZ am Schützenpark
Harmsstr.
Kiel Hbf
Mettenhof, Roskilder Weg
Melsdorfer Feldweg
Kiel-Russee
Hassee, Kolonnenweg
CITTI-PARK
Saarbrückenstr.
Südfriedhof
Hummelwiese
Bf. Melsdorf
Bahnhof Russee
IKEA
Kiel-Hassee CITTI-PARK
Bärenkrog
Stadtrade
Lantziusstr.
Melsdorf
Dahmeweg
Uhlenkrog
Rendsburg, Schleswig, Husum
Gatowweg
Hofkoppel
Rondeel
REWE CENTER
Christianistr.
Redderkamp
Hassee, Marienlust
Russee, Schiefe Horn
Strucksdiek
Waldwiese
Storm
767 Königsförde
Am Taubenkrug
Ihlkatenweg
Russee, Kirche
Rutkamp
PREY
Gärtnerstr.
Krusenrotter Weg
Rendsburger Hof
Streitkamp
Ihlseeweg
Pudelhütte
Am Hain
Speckenbeker Weg
Seekoppelweg
Schleswiger Str.
Diesterwegstr.
Fröbelstr.
Wulfsbrook
Pappelweg
Tannenholz
Petersburger Weg
Wollbergsredder
Rammseer Weg
Schulensee
Hasenholz
Rammsee, Osterberg
Friedhof Osterberg
Eiderbad
Hamburger Baum
Holunderbusch
Krummbogen
Am Voßberg
Wiepenkrog
Eiderbrücke
Meimersdorf
Molfsee, ...
Am Bib
Rammsee, ...
Verwaltung
Flintbek
Kolberg
Schulenhof
Meimersdorf, Am Reben
Bärenkrug
Catharinenberg
Freilichtmuseum
Alte Ziegelei
Mielkendorfer Weg
Sonderbereich
3110
780 Nortorf
790 Flintbek
Neumünster, Hamburg, Fernverkehr
792 Flintbek

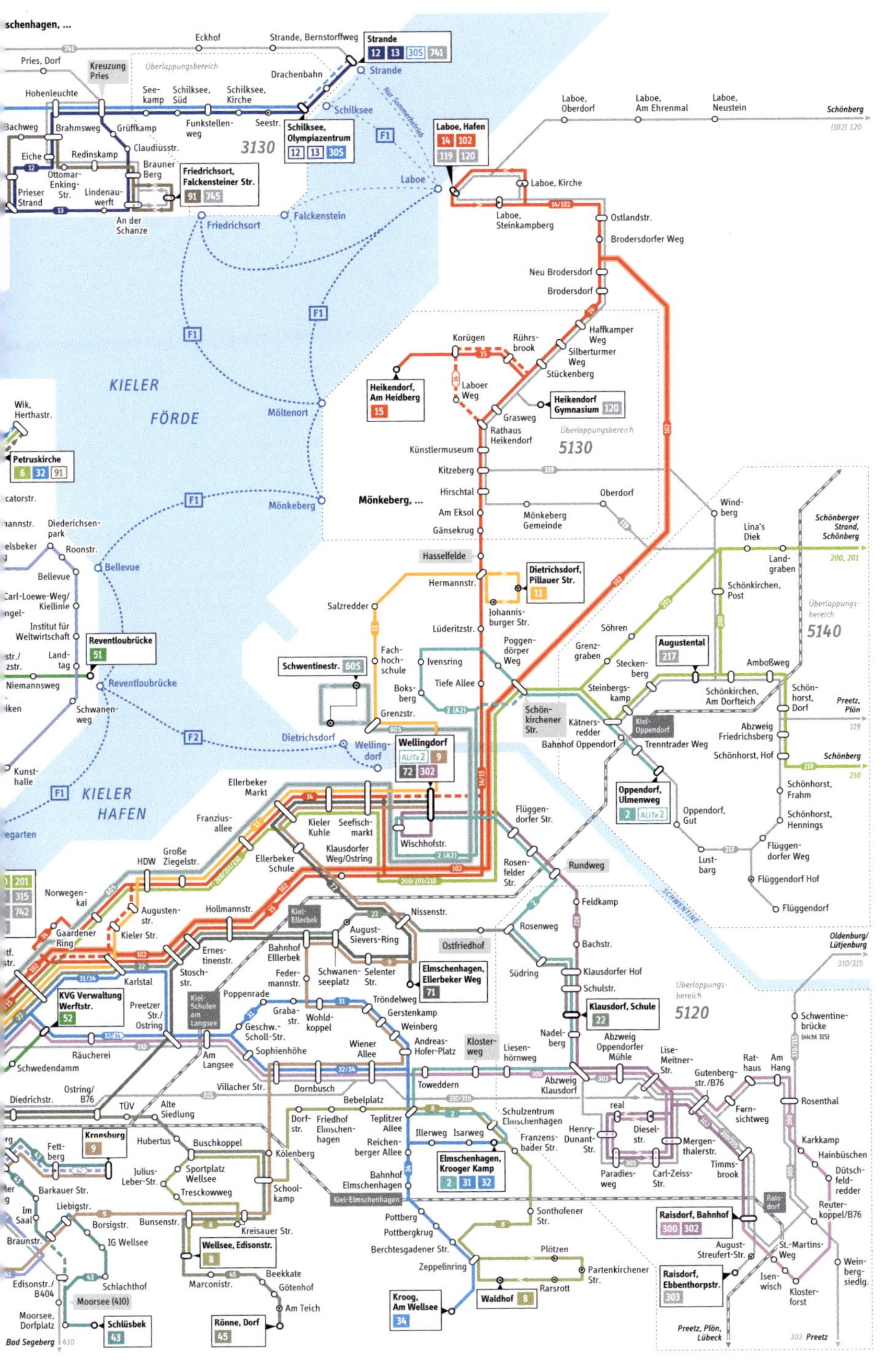

schenhagen, ...
Eckhof
Strande, Bernstorffweg
Strande
12 13 30S 741
Pries, Dorf
Kreuzung Pries
Überlappungsbereich
Drachenbahn
Strande
Hohenleuchte
See-kamp
Schilksee, Süd
Schilksee, Kirche
Schilksee
Nur Sommerbetrieb
Bachweg
Brahmsweg
Grüffkamp
Funkstellen-weg
Seestr.
Schilksee, Olympiazentrum
12 13 30S
3130
Claudiusstr.
Eiche
Redinskamp
F1
Brauner Berg
Ottomar-Enking-Str.
Prieser Strand
Lindenau-werft
Friedrichsort, Falckensteiner Str.
91 745
An der Schanze
Laboe, Hafen
14 102
119 120
Laboe
Friedrichsort
Falckenstein
Laboe, Oberdorf
Laboe, Am Ehrenmal
Laboe, Neustein
Schönberg
[102] 120
Laboe, Kirche
Laboe, Steinkampberg
14/102
Ostlandstr.
Brodersdorfer Weg
Neu Brodersdorf
Brodersdorf
Haffkamper Weg
Silberturmer Weg
Stückenberg
Korügen
Rührs-brook
Heikendorf, Am Heidberg
15
Laboer Weg
Heikendorf Gymnasium
120
Grasweg
Rathaus Heikendorf
Überlappungsbereich
5130
KIELER FÖRDE
Möltenort
Künstlermuseum
Kitzeberg
Hirschtal
Am Eksol
Gänsekrug
Oberdorf
Mönkeberg Gemeinde
Mönkeberg, ...
Mönkeberg
Wik, Herthastr.
Petruskirche
6 32 91
Wind-berg
Lina's Diek
Schönberger Strand, Schönberg
200, 201
Land-graben
Diedrichsen-park
Roonstr.
Bellevue
Bellevue
Carl-Loewe-Weg/ Kiellinie
Institut für Weltwirtschaft
Reventloubrücke
51
Land-tag
Niemannsweg
Reventloubrücke
Schwanen-weg
Hasselfelde
Hermannstr.
Dietrichsdorf, Pillauer Str.
11
Salzredder
Johannis-burger Str.
Lüderitzstr.
Schönkirchen, Post
Überlappungs-bereich
5140
Söhren
Grenz-graben
Augustental
217
Amboßweg
Stecken-berg
Steinbergs-kamp
Schönkirchen, Am Dorfteich
Schön-horst, Dorf
Preetz, Plön
Fach-hoch-schule
Ivensring
Poggen-dörper Weg
Tiefe Allee
Boks-berg
Schwentinestr.
60S
Grenzstr.
Schön-kirchener Str.
Kätners-redder
Kiel-Oppendorf
Bahnhof Oppendorf
Trenntrader Weg
Abzweig Friedrichsberg
Schönhorst, Hof
Schönberg
210
Dietrichsdorf
Welling-dorf
Wellingdorf
ALiTa 2 9
72 302
Oppendorf, Ulmenweg
2 ALiTa 2
Oppendorf, Gut
Schönhorst, Frahm
Schönhorst, Hennings
Kunst-halle
KIELER HAFEN
Ellerbeker Markt
Franzius-allee
Kieler Kuhle
Seefisch-markt
Flüggen-dorfer Str.
Lust-barg
Flüggen-dorfer Weg
Flüggendorf Hof
Flüggendorf
Wischhofstr.
Klausdorfer Weg/Ostring
Rosen-felder Str.
Rundweg
SCHWENTINE
Große Ziegelstr.
HDW
Ellerbeker Schule
Norwegen-kai
201
315
742
Augusten-str.
Kieler Str.
Hollmannstr.
Kiel-Ellerbek
Nissenstr.
Feldkamp
Gaardener Ring
August-Sievers-Ring
Ostfriedhof
Rosenweg
Bachstr.
Ernes-tinenstr.
Bahnhof Ellerbek
Feder-mannstr.
Schwanen-seeplatz
Selenter Str.
Elmschenhagen, Ellerbeker Weg
71
Südring
Klausdorfer Hof
Schulstr.
Oldenburg/ Lütjenburg
310/315
Karlstal
Stosch-str.
KVG Verwaltung Werftstr.
52
Preetzer Str./ Ostring
Kiel-Schulen am Langsee
Poppenrade
Tröndelweg
Gerstenkamp
Weinberg
Klausdorf, Schule
22
Überlappungs-bereich
5120
Graba-str.
Geschw.-Scholl-Str.
Wohld-koppel
Andreas-Hofer-Platz
Kloster-weg
Liesen-hörnweg
Nadel-berg
Abzweig Oppendorfer Mühle
Schwentine-brücke (nicht 315)
Räucherei
Am Langsee
Sophienhöhe
Wiener Allee
Lise-Meitner-Str.
Rat-haus
Am Hang
Schwedendamm
Gutenberg-str./B76
Toweddern
Abzweig Klausdorf
Diedrichstr.
Ostring/ B76
Villacher Str.
Dornbusch
real
Rosenthal
TÜV
Alte Siedlung
Bebelplatz
Schulzentrum Elmschenhagen
Fern-sichtweg
Dorf-str.
Friedhof Elmschen-hagen
Teplitzer Allee
Henry-Dunant-Str.
Diesel-str.
Kronsburg
9
Fett-berg
Hubertus
Buschkoppel
Illerweg
Isarweg
Franzens-bader Str.
Mergen-thalerstr.
Karkkamp
Hainbüschen
Julius-Leber-Str.
Sportplatz Wellsee
Kölenberg
Reichen-berger Allee
Elmschenhagen, Krooger Kamp
2 31 32
Paradies-weg
Carl-Zeiss-Str.
Timms-brook
Dütsch-feld-redder
Barkauer Str.
Tresckowweg
School-kamp
Bahnhof Elmschenhagen
Kiel-Elmschenhagen
Rais-dorf
Im Saal
Liebigstr.
Reuter-koppel/B76
Borsigstr.
Bunsenstr.
Kreisauer Str.
Pottberg
Sonthofener Str.
Raisdorf, Bahnhof
300 302
Braunstr.
IG Wellsee
Wellsee, Edisonstr.
8
Pottbergkrug
Berchtesgadener Str.
August-Streufert-Str.
St.-Martins-Weg
Wein-berg-siedlg.
Schlachthof
Plötzen
Edisonstr./ B404
Moorsee (410)
Marconistr.
Beekkate
Götenhof
Zeppelinring
Partenkirchener Str.
Raisdorf, Ebbenthorpstr.
303
Isen-wisch
Kloster-forst
Rarsrott
Waldhof
8
Am Teich
Kroog, Am Wellsee
34
Moorsee, Dorfplatz
Schlüsbek
43
Rönne, Dorf
45
Preetz, Plön, Lübeck
Bad Segeberg
410
303 Preetz

INDEX

PERSONAL NOTES

Uwe Bogen
Stuttgart
Bildband
144 Seiten
22 x 23 cm, Hardcover
ISBN 978-3-8392-2443-4
€ 20,00 [D] / € 20,60 [A]

Jahr für Jahr entdecken mehr Besucher die Reize der baden-württembergischen Landeshauptstadt, erliegen dem Charme der Kontraste, den Stuttgarts viele Gesichter bilden: Moderne Architektur, jahrhundertealte Prachtbauten, angesagte Szeneviertel, ein buntes kulturelles Spektrum und Weinberge mitten in der Stadt. Stuttgarts Wahrzeichen, der älteste Fernsehturm der Welt, eröffnet den Blick auf eine lebendige Großstadt in ständigem Wandel – und dieser Bildband blickt mitten hinein ins pulsierende Herz der schwäbischen Metropole.

GMEINER

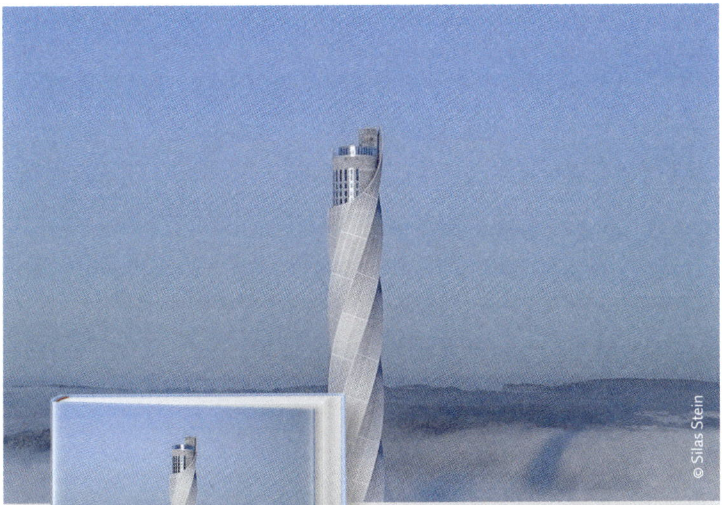

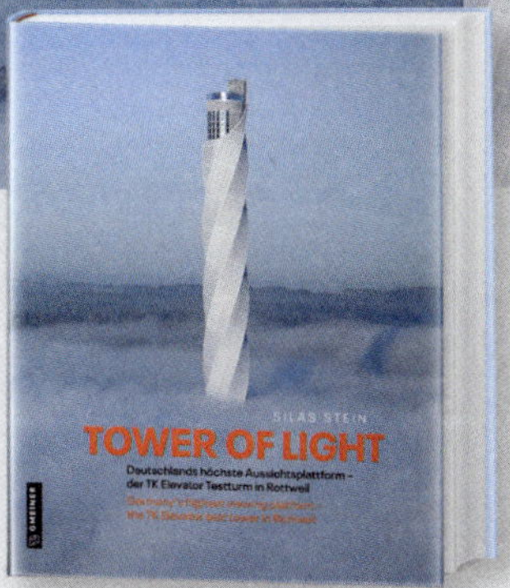

Silas Stein
Tower of Light
Bildband
192 Seiten
22 x 28 cm, Hardcover
ISBN 978-3-8392-0204-3
€ 26,00 [D] / € 26,80 [A]

Der TK Elevator Testturm in Rottweil ist ein Bauwerk der Superlative. Mit seinen 246 Metern besitzt er die höchste Besucherplattform Deutschlands und obendrein einen grandiosen Panoramablick auf Rottweil und die Region. Eigens für die Entwicklung von Hochgeschwindigkeitsaufzügen errichtet, besticht der Bau durch seine unverwechselbare futuristische Silhouette.

Silas Stein, Pressefotograf und gebürtiger Rottweiler, hat die fünfjährige Bauphase des Testturms fotografisch begleitet. In einzigartigen Bildern zeigt er, wie das Gebäude Stück um Stück in den Himmel wächst und beeindruckt mit Aufnahmen des fertigen Turms vor spektakulären Kulissen wie Gewitter und Feuerwerk.